The Revelation of Evolutionary Events
in Myths, Stories, and Legends

by

EveLynn B. Debusschere

Published by:
>   The Association of Waldorf Schools of North America
>   3911 Bannister Road
>   Fair Oaks, CA 95628

The Revelation of Evolutionary Events
in Myths, Stories and Legends

Author: EveLynn B. Debusschere

Editor: David Mitchell

Proofreader: Nancy Jane

© 1997 By AWSNA

ISBN # 1-888365-10-2

>   Curriculum Series

   The Publications Committee of AWSNA is pleased to bring forward this publication as part of its Curriculum Series. The thoughts and ideas represented herein are solely those of the author and do not necessarily represent any implied criteria set by AWSNA. It is our intention to stimulate as much writing and thinking as possible about our curriculum, including diverse views. Please contact us with feedback on this publication as well as requests for future work.

>   David S. Mitchell
>   For the Publications Committee
>   AWSNA

TABLE OF CONTENTS

Introduction	5
The First Three Incarnations	6
The Fourth Incarnation	11
The Seven Days of Creation	12
Lemuria	16
The Norse Myths	18
Atlantis	22
Transition to the Post-Atlantean Epoch	27
Old Indian Epoch	30
Old Persian Epoch	33
The Epic of Gilgamesh	36
Egypto/Chaldean Epoch	40
Osiris - Isis	41
Abraham - Isaac	45
Transition to Intellectual Soul Age: Jacob - Joseph	48
The Greek Myths	53
Aeneas	58
Moses	60
Greco/Roman Epoch	61
The Arthurian Legends	65
Consciousness Soul Age	72
Parzival	74
A Modern Myth	80
Epilogue	82
References	84
Bibliography	92
Description of Illustrations	93

INTRODUCTION

Rudolf Steiner describes the human being as consisting of three aspects – physical, soul, and spirit – each of which is further differentiated into three finer aspects. The physical consists of the physical body, the etheric body, and the astral body. The soul is differentiated into the sentient, intellectual, and consciousness soul. The spirit contains the Spirit-Self, Life-Spirit, and Spirit-Man.[1]

The evolution of these members of the human being is connected with the evolution of the earth. Through spiritual research and a reading of the "abiding traces of all spiritual happenings,"[2] called the "Akashic Records," Steiner is able to give us a picture of the earth's evolution. The earth is a living entity, and as such has gone through and has yet to go through various "incarnations" of its evolution. "Our earth evolution can only have meaning, if during its course something arises which was not there before. A perpetual repetition of what was already there would be a meaningless existence. Through the coming into existence of the earth something new became possible; it became possible for man to become man as we know him."[3] The facts of cosmic evolution repeat themselves in humanity's inner knowledge and are revealed in myths, legends, and stories of various cultures.

To begin with, a "map" or outline of Steiner's indications of the earth's evolution will be helpful, and from there a description of each of the earth's "incarnations" will follow. In total the earth will incarnate seven times, each incarnation divided into seven smaller cycles, each with their own seven small subdivisions. These seven times sevenfold divisions are more distinct in the fourth evolution of the earth, the present evolution, and are less distinct the further one goes back in history.[4] A time of rest, "pralaya," exists in between each incarnation and each new incarnation begins with a recapitulation of that which has already taken place, but this recapitulation represents a higher stage of development than that of the former embodiment.

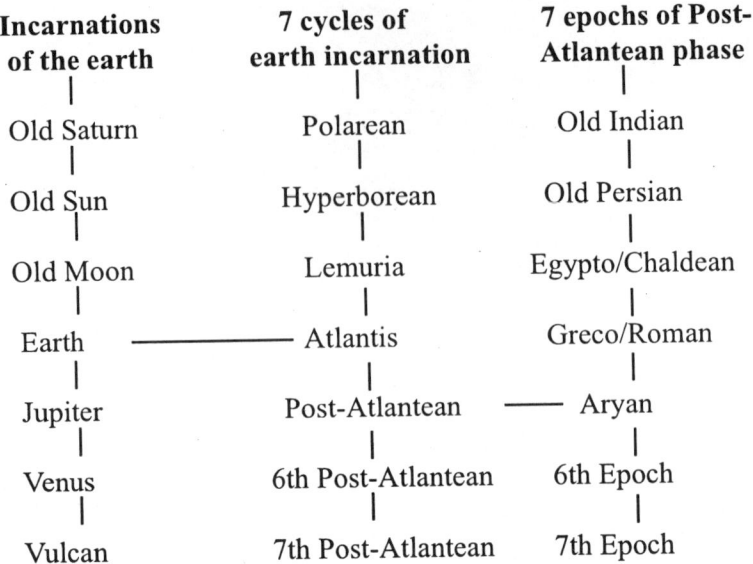

Using Rudolf Steiner's indications of the evolution of earth, a picture can be built of the first four incarnations of the earth, the first five cycles of the Earth incarnation, and the first five epochs of the Post-Atlantean cycle, which will bring us to our present time. Since man is the goal of the evolution of the earth,[5] an exploration of stories, myths and legends, beginning with the story of creation, will give a reflection of the development of the human being and humanity.

THE FIRST THREE INCARNATIONS

The first incarnation of the earth is designated as Old Saturn. On Old Saturn, the "germ" of the physical body of mankind existed; the oldest member of the human being is the physical body, and it is this body that has attained the greatest degree of perfection. Yet this body of Old Saturn was not as we know it today; the germ of the physical body was but the first rudiment of the later physical body, and consisted of nothing but an interweaving of "warmth." In the first cycle of Old Saturn, the development of this primitive body with a dull, trance-like consciousness began. Following this cycle, there were six other cycles, and during these subsequent cycles mankind did not attain a higher degree of consciousness, but rather, through the work of higher spiritual beings, the material body was further elaborated. During the second cycle of Old Saturn, the human body was worked on in such a way that a "wise arrangement," a rational structure, was implanted in it, and in the third cycle, the capacity for movement and forceful activity was implanted. During the fourth cycle, the human body, which until now was like a mobile cloud, received a bounded form, while in the fifth cycle, the germs of the sensory organs were implanted. At this time selfhood was also implanted into the body, and without this, humanity would never become a self-enclosed entity, a "personality." In the next cycle, the sense organs that were implanted in the previous cycle were enlivened, and humanity rose to a kind of shining entity. In the last cycle of Old Saturn a kind of understanding was developed, yet in this stage of dull consciousness, humanity was unable to make use of it. On Old Saturn, the human being matured to the point of beginning to develop the predisposition to spiritual man, the seed of Spirit-Man, the highest member of man that will reach full development only at the end of the development of mankind[6] in the Vulcan incarnation of the earth.

The "physical body on Old Saturn was a delicate, tenuous, ethereal body-of-warmth, and the entire Saturn consisted of these warmth-bodies. They were the first beginnings of the present physical-mineral body of man."[7] Everything that existed on Old Saturn was in a mineral condition or form, but not of the mineral condition that we know today. Old Saturn was nothing but interweaving warmth, but the laws that prevailed were the same laws which are present today in the solid mineral kingdom; it can be said that Old Saturn was a "state of interweaving warmth governed by mineral laws."[8]

At the end of the seventh cycle, the Old Saturn evolution died away, and the seed of man passed into a state of rest, waiting to be worked on again in the next earth incarnation.

After a period of rest, the second incarnation of the earth, designated as Old Sun, began with a rapid recapitulation of what took place during Old Saturn, but a repetition that was adapted to the changed conditions of Old Sun. The physical body unfolded, and when the degree of evolution that was attained on Old Saturn had been adapted to the new conditions, the etheric or life-body was poured into the physical body. The physical body was permeated by a second, more delicate body, the ether body, and the nature of the physical body was changed in order to carry this new body.[9] During the remaining cycles of Old Sun, the etheric body was developed further and through forces which acted on the physical body, and the physical body became more perfect.[10] The etheric body reached its first level of perfection and the physical body its second level of perfection. With the permeation of the physical body by the etheric body, humanity became an animated being; life began to be. During Old Sun, the physical body and the etheric body separated into two distinct parts, although the physical body remained permeated by the life-body. Thus, there was the beginning of a two-fold nature of the human being.[11]

During Old Sun, a denser, gaseous element was added to the interweaving warmth, and a radiation of light ascended into space. At this time, planetary evolution had advanced to the stage of the plant, but not as in the present form. The multitude of plant forms that exist today pervaded Old Sun as group-souls or species. In the warmth and the gaseous elements, the same laws were at work that rule the plant kingdom today, laws that determine that blossoms will grow upwards and roots will grow downwards.[12] Alongside the mineral realm there was a plant realm.

Mankind evolved to a plant-like consciousness on Old Sun, living a plant existence with a consciousness that had the quality of dreamless sleep. During the second cycle of Old Sun, the etheric body was able to bring inner movement to the physical body, movements that are comparable to the flowing of saps and fluids in plants today.[13] The rudiments of the head of the physical body pointed downwards as the roots of the plants do today, while the rudiments of the feet pointed upwards like the blossoms of the plants of today.[14]

Through the cycles of Old Sun the gaseous structures assumed more permanent shapes; the previously cloudlike mobility of the ether body maintained a more distinguishable form. The first suggestions of a reproductive process arose, and the sensory germs of Old Saturn were transformed into animated senses. During the last cycle of this earth incarnation, the human being was able to feel the first hints of sympathy and antipathy with the surrounding environment. This was not yet true feeling, but it was the forerunner of feeling. There was also a kind of primitive speech – an outward expression of an inward perception through sound.[15] As the seed of Spirit-Man was implanted on Old Saturn, so, too, was the first seed of Life-Spirit formed on Old Sun. This will develop in the second last, the Venus incarnation of the earth.

During Old Sun, Saturn separated off. At the end of the Old Sun incarnation, a period of rest again followed, and all that evolved on Old Sun went into a state of rest, waiting to emerge when a new planetary existence began. During this interval of rest, Saturn reunited with the earth, only to separate again during the recapitulation of Old Sun in the following incarnation of the earth.

The planetary evolution that emerged after Old Sun, designated as Old Moon, began with another repetition of the Old Saturn and Old

Sun events. The physical life of man repeated the stages of development from Old Saturn, but now under new conditions, until in the last of the Old Saturn repetition, the human being had the appearance that was there on Old Sun. The inpouring of the etheric body into the physical body was then repeated.[16] This repetition was not a mere reenactment of the events that took place on Old Saturn and Old Sun. The development of the physical body and the etheric body transformed these two bodies of the human being so that they could be united with a third body, the astral body, the basis of consciousness.[17] When this third body entered the human being, the physical body was raised to its third level of perfection, and the etheric body was raised to its second level of perfection.[18] With the inpouring of the astral body, humanity acquired the first qualities of soul. The beginning of feelings that developed on Old Sun were transformed, and the first indications of wish and craving existed, but this craving appeared to be instinctive. When the astral was poured into the warmth and gaseous body, the physical condensed further to a liquid state. For the first time the human physical body had three elements that were distinct from each other. The densest "watery" body was permeated by airy currents and warmth.[19]

The development of the human astral body was connected with a great cosmic event that took place during Old Moon. In the third cycle of Old Moon, the previously single heavenly body separated into two bodies; one part became the sun, and the other remained the earth. The new born sun took with it elements of air and warmth and began to send its forces to the earth from without.[20] These forces were not physical light alone, but rather light ensouled, inspirited by the force of love.[21] As a result of this, the living beings of Old Moon could "take into themselves astral bodies and so develop consciousness, reflect in inner experience what went on around them. An animal nature, an inwardly living animal nature, a nature capable of consciousness, is dependent for its existence upon separation between sun and earth elements. The animal nature first appeared during the Moon evolution."[22]

During the time of Old Moon, the human being developed the third of his seven states of consciousness. On Old Saturn there was a dull, trance like consciousness. Old Sun consciousness was like the state of dreamless sleep. Old Moon consciousness was like dream-filled sleep,[23] a form of clairvoyance or picture consciousness where images that were related to objects and beings of the outside world arose within the human being. There was as yet no distinction between inner and outer experiences. There existed a pictorial consciousness that was permeated with the quality of inwardness, and where no faculty of discrimination was yet possible.[24] The images that arose within the human being were capable of arousing inner life to movement and action. "The inner processes took shape to accord with [the images], they were formative forces in the true sense of the word. The human being became even as they formed him. He became, so to speak, the image of his own processes in consciousness."[25] The human being of Old Moon was scarcely aware of anything except what was happening to himself.[26] Furthermore, as Old Moon moved about the sun, there developed two states of consciousness, one more predominant when closer to the sun and one more predominant while further from the sun. The alternation in these two states of consciousness is similar to the alternation between sleeping and waking today.[27]

During Old Saturn, there existed only warmth, which became denser during Old Sun to form air, and which also became finer to form light. During Old Moon, while the elements condensed further to form a watery state, the light ascended to a finer element of sound ether.[28] Mankind "had to sink the formerly luminous gas-form into the turbid waters and incarnate there as ... water-form, but not entirely. Never did [mankind] descend entirely into the water."[29] Mankind was a half-vapor, half-water being. The sound ether or tone that ascended from the light was a shaping power, and it was this power that formed the vapor being of mankind. In the vapor-body that rose above the surface of the water, mankind still participated in the forces of light and love that streamed in from the spiritual world. This upper part was transformed to become suited for something new, for the breathing of air. Now that which streamed down as divine forces was divided into two parts, air, which penetrated mankind as breath and light. With the first drawing of breath, the consciousness of birth and death entered into [mankind]. "... The air-breath, which had split off from its brother the light ray, and which thereby had split off also the beings who earlier had flowed in with the light, had brought death to [mankind]."[30]

The animal realm joined the plant and mineral realms.[31] Amid all of these influences, the human being developed to the point where he began "to develop within him the seed of Spirit-Self, just as the seed of Spirit-Man arose in the second half of Saturn evolution and the seed of Life-Spirit on Sun."[32] This seed of Spirit-Self will develop in the next earth incarnation, the Jupiter incarnation.

As Old Moon drew to a close, the sun and earth reunited, and the seven Old Moon cycles with their intervening periods of rest came to an end. There was a stage of sleep until the fourth incarnation of the earth began.

THE FOURTH INCARNATION

During the first three incarnations of the earth, the components of the lower nature of the human being were formed - the physical body, the etheric body. and the astral body. With the introduction of each new body, the old ones were changed so that they could become carriers for the new body. When the human being gained the etheric body, he was able to feel joy and pain, and with the introduction of the astral body, emotions of rage, hate, and love were experienced. When there existed only a physical body, human beings had only a dull consciousness, developing a state of dreamless sleep with the arrival of the etheric body, and a state of dreaming consciousness with the formation of the astral body. While the lower nature of the human being was being developed, so, too, was the higher nature - Spirit-Man, Life-Spirit, and Spirit-Self. Thus, two origins of man were being developed simultaneously during the three great cosmic cycles of Old Saturn, Old Sun, and Old Moon. The Earth incarnation serves to bring these two separate origins of the human being together.[33]

During Old Moon "what man was supposed to become was clothed in a warm astral sheath, and it is this part which on Earth enables the inner human life to develop love from the lowest to the highest form."[34] The task or mission of the Earth incarnation is to develop love, that force which came streaming in from the sun, when it separated from the earth during Old Moon.

As at the beginning of the previous earth incarnations, the fourth incarnation of the earth began with a recapitulation of the first three. It is at this point in time that stories, myths, and legends can be looked at for revelations of cosmic events and the development of humanity. In his book, *Genesis*, Rudolf Steiner brings to light the reflection of the recapitulation of Old Saturn, Old Sun, and Old Moon in the story of the seven days of creation found in the first book of the Bible; "all that is narrated in the Bible of the six or seven 'days' of creation is a reawakening of previous conditions, not in the same but in a new form."[35]

THE SEVEN DAYS OF CREATION

First of all, the meaning of "day" throughout the time of creation must be examined. "Day" cannot mean the twenty-four hour day that depends upon the relationship of the earth to the sun, for the sun did not exist until the fourth "day" of creation. Each "day" represents a great cosmic cycle of time, cosmic history, which Steiner describes as the time appointed to the specific Time-Spirits to carry out their work, followed by a period of rest. "There was a state of disorder, and it was followed by a state of order, of harmony, brought out by the work of the ... Time Spirits."[36] This is the meaning of "morning" and "evening."

The beginning of Genesis is the beginning of the Earth incarnation and the story of creation reflects all that had taken place during Old Saturn, Old Sun, and Old Moon, emerging again in a new form. Steiner describes the opening words of the Bible, "In the beginning of creation, when God made heaven and earth," (Gen.1:1), as a picture of the spiritual beings who were involved with the evolution of earth musing over or recollecting what had transpired so far, and in the meditative work of these spiritual beings, two complexes arose, one tending towards external revelation, external manifestation, and another consisting of an inward stimulus, an inward life. Herein lies the meaning of "heaven and earth." These two arising complexes were in a state which is designated as "the earth was without form and void, with darkness over the face of abyss" (Gen.1:2).[37] The earth was still in darkness, for the sun was as yet still enclosed within it and was not without radiating upon it.

As the Earth incarnation began with the recapitulation of the previous incarnations, one would expect to see the recapitulation of Old Saturn in the story of creation - the presence of Old Saturn warmth. This appears in the words "and a mighty wind that swept over the surface of the waters" (Gen.1:2). This mighty wind is the "brooding" of Old Saturn warmth, the radiating of the warmth of Old Saturn over the other elementary states.[38] So in these first words of Genesis, there is revealed the recapitulation of Old Saturn in its new form. This is the Polarean cycle, the first of the seven cycles of the Earth incarnation. This image of the recapitulation of Old Saturn can also be seen in the creation myths of the Norse myths. In the beginning, the world consisted of two realms, Muspell, the region with dancing flames, and Niflheim, a realm of ice and snow. In between the two lay a "huge and seeming emptiness, Ginnungagap. In the middle of Ginnungagap the warmth of Muspell met the cold of Niflheim and there life began."[39]

As the Earth incarnation is meant to bring the higher and lower nature of the human being together, one must look to see how this is to come about. Rudolf Steiner says that on the first day of creation, the sentient soul was being prepared. At the beginning of the physical Earth, there was a soul-form encircling the sphere of the earth surrounded by warmth. "As a consequence of this envelopment by warmth, not only is life kindled in the human being, but at the same time a change takes place in his astral body. Into it is implanted the first beginning of that which afterwards becomes the sentient soul. We may say therefore, that at this stage, man consists of sentient soul, astral body, life-body, and a physical body that is woven of fire."[40] During the recapitulation of Old Saturn, the physical body was worked on so that it would be able to receive the more highly evolved etheric body when it unfolded.[41]

The beginning of the recapitulation of Old Sun is revealed in Genesis with the words: "God said, 'Let there be light', and there was light" (Gen.1:3). During Old Sun, when the airy or gaseous element descended from the warmth, the light ascended from the warmth. However, the light referred to here in Genesis is not merely a repeat of what occurred on Old Sun, but rather it is something new that happens; "the Elohim did not merely feel themselves to be flowing with the light, but that light streamed back to them from objects,"[42] and what was previously experienced subjectively was now manifested without, and "God saw that the light was good" (Gen.1:4) - an inner spiritual element revealed itself in an external form.[43]

During the recapitulation of Old Sun the etheric body was developed further, and also a portion of the astral body separated to form the first germinal beginnings of the intellectual soul,[44] and within the circumference of the earth there existed the sentient soul and the intellectual soul.

So we come to the end of the first day of creation, and the end of the recapitulation of Old Sun, the end of the Hyperborean cycle of the Earth incarnation.

The second day of creation tells of the separation of "water from water" (Gen.1:6). Here the sound-ether or tone that had ascended from the light during Old Moon began to organize the elementary substances, so that within the waters one element tended to condense into something "watery," and one element elevated into vapor. The second day of creation reveals the beginning of the recapitulation of Old Moon, the Lemurian age.

On the third day of creation, God gathered the water into one place so that dry land appeared - water was separated from something that had not existed before, the solid element. During Old Moon this solid element was not in existence, but in the recapitulation of Old Moon it precipitated out of water; the earth element emerged as something new. This new earth element brought about the recapitulation of the plant nature. The etheric body that came into being during Old Moon reappeared in the Earth incarnation, and the earth produced fresh growth and "plants bearing seed according to their kind and trees bearing fruit each with seed according to its kind" (Gen.1:12). The phrase "according to its kind" refers to the existence of species of plants, not individual plants as we see them today. With the entering of the life-forces, life began to stir on earth.

The astral body of man developed further, and man advanced to the stage of consciousness soul; with the incorporation of the watery element, the consciousness soul was added to the first beginnings of the sentient soul and the intellectual soul.[45] The soul-spiritual being of man, the beginnings of the three aspects of the soul along with the Spirit-Man, Life-Spirit, and Spirit-Self, continued to hover in the periphery of the earth. As the human being continued to evolve, this soul-spiritual element of man gradually became clothed in a body.

On the fourth day of creation "God said, 'Let there be lights in the vault of heaven to separate day from night and let them serve as signs both for festivals and for seasons, and years. Let them also shine in the vault of heaven to give light on earth'" (Gen.1:14). This is the repetition of the separation of the sun that had taken place during Old Moon, again a repetition with something new. During the Lemurian age another great event took place that gave evolution a new turn, for this was the time when our present moon left the earth,[46] and the earth found a balance between the sun and the moon and at last came into its own.[47] The earth "evolved from a unity to a duality to a trinity: sun, earth, and moon."[48] On the fourth day of creation "God made the two great lights, the greater to govern the day and the lesser to govern the night; and with them he made the stars" (Gen.1:16). This places the fourth day of creation after the exit of the moon. Both the sun and the moon withdrew from the earth, "and in this way the earth prepared itself to become the bearer of human existence."[49] Not only did the sun and moon come into being at this time, but also the activity of the stars. Cosmic existence was added to earthly existence. The first influences which formed the astral body of mankind streamed in from the world of the stars, as the stars unfolded their activity in the periphery of the earth. With this new activity, on the fourth day of creation, the soul-spiritual nature of mankind clothed itself in the laws and forces of the astral body.[50]

When the sun first separated from the earth during Old Moon, the light streaming onto earth from without allowed for the first appearance of the animal nature; "in order for anything animal to find a place on earth, there had to be a repetition of the being shone upon, an influence of forces acting from without."[51] When this event was repeated during the fourth day of creation, there followed a recapitulation of the animal nature in the earth element, now in a new form, at a higher level of development. Accordingly, on the fifth day of creation "God said, 'Let the waters teem with countless living creatures, and let birds fly above the earth across the vault of heaven'" (Gen.1:20), and God created creatures according to their own kind, not individual animals, but species of animals.

At the end of the fifth day of creation, all of the necessary recapitulations had occurred for something new to begin. On the sixth day of creation, creatures whose existence was bound to the new earth element appeared - "cattle, reptiles, and wild animals, all according to their kind" (Gen.1:24). Once this was done, a new form was available to serve the human form, the consummation of the work of evolution, and "God said, 'Let us make man'" (Gen.1:26). At that time the physical body of man came into existence, not in a solid fleshy form, but only as the first manifestation of the physical, as a being of warmth and air.[52] "In the image of God he created him; male and female he created them" (Gen.1:27). The first image of the human being combined both sexes, and this hermaphroditic humanity had the capacity to propagate, for God told them to "be fruitful and increase" (Gen.1:28). This "signifies that as a result of the soul-spiritual element still holding sway over the bodily element, it was possible for the first earth man to produce his like from within, to build bodily sheaths for other human beings."[53]

"On the sixth day God completed all the work he had been doing, and on the seventh day he ceased from all his work" (Gen.2:2) - ceased from the work of creation.[54]

After these seven days of creation, Genesis describes a second creation of man: "Then the Lord God formed a man from the dust of the ground" (Gen.2:7). Rudolf Steiner describes this as the aspect of the moon that remained in the human being after the moon separated from the earth, and God "imprinted into man the earth-dust."[55] From there the human body was endowed with something, for God "breathed into his nostrils the breath of life. Thus man became a living creature" (Gen.2:7), and with this "breath of life" the human being gained the beginnings of the physical body that we find today.[56] That which "was previously spiritual [was] imprinted into the body as the breath of life."[57] Something from without entered into the human being to unite with the bodily nature. That which entered was the soul-spiritual nature that was prepared during the first three days of creation - the sentient soul, the intellectual soul, and the consciousness soul along with the Spirit-Man, Life-Spirit, and Spirit-Self – and "the 'I' was kindled in him."[58]

The human being that was first formed on the sixth day of creation continued to evolve and separated into male and female beings - Adam and Eve. This was an important development for humankind, for the forces that were previously used for reproduction from within were now freed. These forces became available to form a thinking brain; "by impregnating each other, human beings can turn a part of their productive energy within and so become thinking creatures."[59] This thinking brain became the mediator with the spirit, and the human being became the spiritual being that he is today. With the division into sexes a new impulse awoke in the soul - the desire for knowledge. Another new impulse was selfishness.[60] Adam and Eve do not represent two individuals, but rather they symbolize the humanity that existed during Lemuria.

LEMURIA

After the days of creation, humanity did not yet walk upon the surface of the earth but still remained within the periphery of the earth. The fall out of Paradise down onto the surface of the earth came through the Luciferic influence, the temptation of Eve by the serpent. The story of the fall from Paradise depicts the point in evolution when humanity yielded to the allurement of new consciousness - the desire for knowledge - which "in the inner life of imagination and ideation, the female human being had already approached more closely,"[61] and Eve ate of

the tree of knowledge of good and evil (Gen.3:6). As a result of the Luciferic influence, the body of the human being condensed further, and the body of flesh came into being "and they discovered that they were naked" (Gen.3:7) - Adam and Eve lost their light filled body, the body of which they were made in the 'image of God', and they gained a dense physical body. This body was heavier and sank out of the earth's periphery, out of Paradise, to the surface of the earth and for the first time acquired the force of gravity.[62] Had these events not taken place, the ego that humanity had received in a germinal form would have come to full fruition in the middle of the earth evolution, but such an ego would not have been free. Through the influence of the Luciferic beings in the Lemurian age, mankind was endowed with freedom, the freedom to choose between good and evil. Through eating the apple, mankind came to self-consciousness and knowledge prematurely.[63]

At the expulsion from Paradise, God set the cherubim with "a sword whirling and flashing" (Gen.3:24), a flaming sword, to end life in Paradise. The Lemurian age "came to an end in a series of great catastrophes resulting from volcanic activity,"[64] and those human beings who could, saved "themselves by taking refuge on some region of the Earth that had so far been protected from the harmful influence of men."[65] The end of Paradise also marks the end of cosmic time and the beginning of mythological time.

Rudolf Steiner gives a picture of the character of the third root race - those who lived during the Lemurian age. Although ideas existed, memory was not yet developed so ideas did not remain in memory. Language was not needed as the people communicated through thoughts. The people understood the "inner nature" of the objects in their environment, and the faculty of imagination was similar to instinct. They had power over their own body, being able to increase strength through the use of will.

The goal of the Lemurian age was to develop the will and the faculty of imagination. The will was mainly developed by the males and the imagination through the females. This faculty of imagination became the basis for a higher development of the life of ideas, forming the germs of memory and the capacity to form the first and simplest moral concepts, which came into being towards the end of the Lemurian age. From the women the first ideas of "good and evil" arose, as depicted in the story of Eve eating the apple. Thus, the development that was connected with the life of the imagination, with the formation of memory, of customs which formed the seeds for a life of law, for a kind of morals, came through the women. The men became characters of strong will, and through the soul of woman, the willful nature, the vigorous strength of man, was ennobled and refined.

The human body at that time had pliant qualities and changed form whenever the inner life changed, and animal life was subject to even greater changeability. Mighty volcanoes existed throughout Lemuria, and men dealt with this fiery activity in everything they did.[66] Not all beings had developed to the same level at this time, and Steiner refers to the descendants of the "more advanced human beings" mingling with the "less advanced human beings."[67]

THE NORSE MYTHS

Just as we saw the recapitulation of Old Saturn in the Norse myths, so, too, can we find other reflections of life during the Lemurian age in these myths. Referring again to the creation myth, the world was cre-

ated by Odin and his brothers: they shaped the earth with mountains and rocks; they created lakes and seas and surrounded the earth with the rocking ocean; they stretched the sky to cover the earth and placed the sun, moon, and stars high in Ginnungagap to light heaven above and earth below. Jotunheim was made for the giants, and Midgard, where the ground grew green with sprouting leeks, for men. In the air clouds were formed. From two trees, first man and first woman were created, and "Odin breathed into them the spirit of life."[68] Other gifts given to humanity were sharp wits and feeling hearts, and the senses of hearing and sight. Night and Day were set in chariots to ride across the sky, guided by the sun and the moon. Then Dwarfs were made to live under the hills. Thus, the earth was made and filled with men, giants and dwarfs, with the gods in Aesir; the realms of the gods and men were connected by Bifrost - a rainbow bridge. These pictures echo the pictures found in the first chapters of Genesis, reflecting again the evolution of the earth and the development of mankind.

Odin's two ravens, "Havens (Thought) and Muninn (Memory),"[69] show that the people of this age do not yet contain these faculties within themselves. When Loki returns from searching for Mjollnir, Thor's hammer, which he had lost, Thor stops him and says, "Stand here and tell me the truth at once. A sitting man forgets his story as often as not, and a man who lies down first lies again afterwards."[70] When Freya is told the ancestry of Ottar the Young and Angantyr by Hyndla, she asks that Ottar be given the "memory-beer", so that he will remember Hyndla's recital.[71] These images reflect the incapacity for the people of Lemuria to hold ideas within memory.

The pliancy and changeability of the human form is shown throughout the myths. Loki, who is often referred to as "Shape - Changer," takes on the form of a falcon when he dons Frigga's dress of falcon feathers, and he changes Iduna into a sparrow (or in some versions, a nut) when he rescues her from Thiassi,[72] and he changes himself into a mare in order to draw Svaldlfari away from helping the Giant build the wall around Asgard.[73] Odin as well takes on a variety of forms as he travels throughout the world, appearing as "a man to men and a giant to giants."[74]

Likewise the fiery element that had to be dealt with in Lemuria is also apparent in the myths. Jotunheim, the land of the giants, is a land of great mountains that is lighted by "columns of fire thrown up now and again through cracks in the earth or out of the peaks of mountains."[75] In rescuing Iduna, Loki flies through the flames of a great fire which then traps Thiassi his pursuer.[76] Skirnir, in trying to win Gerda for Frey, must ride through a wall of fire in order to gain entrance to her home,[77] and, similarly, Odin has a Hall built for Brynhild, putting a "wall of mounting and circling fire" around it, and through this fire a hero without fear must ride in order to claim her for his bride.[78] Not only are the astral forces of Lemuria visible in the external world of the Norse myths, they are also visible in the "fiery" tempers of the Gods.

Within the Norse myths the desire for knowledge, the new impulse that came with the division into male and female beings, is also reflected. Odin travels to the land of the Giants seeking to learn something from them - the price that he will have to pay for a draught from the Well of Wisdom. Even when he learns that this will cost him his right eye, Odin searches for Mimir, the guardian of the Well of Wisdom and asks to let him drink from the well. After he drinks, "he put his hand to this face and he plucked out his right eye. Terrible was the pain that Odin All-Father endured. But he made no groan nor moan."[79]

However, having gained immense knowledge from Mimir's well, he also wins "with it the thirst for yet greater wisdom," and so he approaches Yggdrasill, the tree that formed the axis of the world, and upon the tree he hangs for nine long nights, and his wisdom grows.[80]

The story of Kvasir also reflects the thirst for knowledge of the Lemurian age. Kvasir is a poet who has wisdom. Two Dwarfs kill him and keep his blood, for in having his blood, they have his wisdom, and no one can have it but them. With it they brew a Magic Mead. These Dwarfs are later captured by the Giant Suttung, and they offer him their Magic Mead in exchange for their freedom. Odin then sets "out to get the Magic Mead [from Suttung] that he might give it to men, so that, tasting it, they would have wisdom, and words would be at their command that would make wisdom loved and remembered."[81]

The trials and conquests of the gods, giants, dwarfs, and men show the development of the will through the men of the age of Lemuria; undergoing danger, overcoming pain, and accomplishing daring deeds hardens and strengthens their will. There are, however, within the collection of Norse myths, two myths in particular that reveal that which was developed through the women. In the story of Geirrod and Agnar, Odin takes Geirrod into his charge and teaches him how to fish and hunt and gives him tasks to make him bolder. On the other hand, Frigga favors Agnar, and he spends time with her, listening to her tales and to the answers to his questions, "learning greatly from her of wisdom and courage and gentleness towards his fellow men."[82] Through what he learns from Frigga, Agnar resolves to "give all his life and all his strength and all his thought to helping the work of the Gods."[83] Geirrod wants to be a hero and a king; he tries to kill Agnar so that he can be the king instead of Agnar. Believing that he has succeeded, Geirrod takes over the kingdom. He becomes a cruel ruler, using the gifts of the Gods to become like a wild beast instead of putting them to noble use. For this, he dies. However, Agnar survives, and using the gifts he received from Frigga, he becomes a kind, strong, and victorious ruler.

In the second story, "Frigga and the Gift of Flax,"[84] a peasant meets Frigga in a cavern filled with glittering gems and gold, while she stands with a small bunch of blue flowers in her hands. She offers him anything that is in the cavern, and he asks only for the flowers that she is holding. She is pleased with his choice, handing him the flowers and a bag of seeds, telling him to sow the seeds and to take good care of the plants that grow from them. He does this, and when the seeds have grown and the plants begin to yellow, Frigga returns to the peasant to show him what he must do with the flax to bring him prosperity; she shows the peasant's wife how to weave linen from the fibres of the plants, and then blessing them she leaves once again. From the peasant and his wife, their children learn the secret that Frigga taught them, and the "flax fields flourished for the good of [the] family for many generations," carrying the gifts of Frigga into the future.

The story of "How Loki Outwitted a Giant"[85] portrays the inner knowingness and instinctive imagination of the people of Lemuria. A Giant, having won a game of chess with a peasant, claims the peasant's son as his prize. When the peasant pleads to be left his son, the Giant agrees to do so if the parents can hide their son where the Giant cannot find him. Three times, with the help of the Gods, the peasant and his wife hide their son, but each time, whether he is a kernel of wheat hidden amongst a wheat field, a swan feather hidden on the breast of a swan, or a tiny fish egg hidden in the roe of a flounder, the Giant, "having some strange knowledge," finds the boy; the inner knowingness of the Giant shows him in each situation where the boy has been hidden by the Gods.

Heimdall, the guardian of Bifrost, also portrays this knowingness of Lemuria. He is described as being able to hear the sound of grass growing and the sound of wool growing on a sheep's back, and he is able to see around him for a hundred miles.[86] For the Lemurian man, knowledge flowed "directly from the objects which surrounded him. It flowed to him from the energy of growth of plants, from the life force of animals."[87]

Two other myths need to be looked at before the end of Lemuria is explored - "Foreboding in Asgard," and "Baldur's Doom."[88] Once when Loki and Odin are travelling through the world of Men, Loki kills Hreidmar's son, Otter. In choosing an offering of recompense for the death of Otter, Odin does not think of offering wisdom, but instead offers gold - a treasure that is guarded by Andvari, a Dwarf. In telling Loki to get the gold from Andvari, Odin's word sets free Gulveig, a Giant woman who had once blighted the early happiness of the Gods and who had been cast out of Asgard. Since Odin and Loki bought their freedom with gold, Gulveig is once again free to enter Asgard. Sadly, Odin returns to Asgard, knowing that Gulveig is following, and where she smiles, Care and Foreboding come, and the thoughts of the Gods begin to change. This is the beginning of the end of Asgard. Odin slays Gulveig in Asgard, "where slaying is forbidden" and has her body burned - but her heart is not devoured by the flames, and Loki eats Gulveig's heart, growing to hate the Gods more and more. Evil and decadence are alive in Asgard as the end of Lemuria draws near.

Through Loki's hatred for the Gods, Baldur, Odin's son, the beautiful young sun-god, is killed. Although the Gods try to have Hela take a ransom for him, Baldur must remain in Hela's hall. Baldur the beautiful is dead, and the joy and content of Asgard are gone. In the story of the death of Baldur, there is an advance reflection of the Christ event.

So, Ragnarok, the Twilight of the Gods, comes to the Dwellers of Asgard, and a great war is raged so that "the powers of evil would be destroyed forever,"[89] even though it also means the end of the world. Odin is devoured by Fenris the Wolf; Thor is killed by Jormungand the monstrous sea serpent; Loki slays Heimdal and is slain by him; and Garm the hound with bloody jaws slays Tyr. The riders of Muspellheim arrive, and Surtur casts fire upon the earth, and Yggdrassill, the World Tree, is burned; the "fire from Muspellheim would sweep over all, and thus would everything be destroyed; and it would indeed be the end of all things."[90]

When the fire ceased, four of the younger Gods stood on the world's highest peak. They were Vida and Vali, Modi and Magni. Baldur and Hodur return from Hela's habitation, and the six together remember what had taken place before Ragnarok. Two humans had saved themselves from the destruction of Ragnarok by hiding themselves deep within Yggdrasill where Surtur's fire could not reach them, and when they awoke, the world was green and beautiful again, and from their children came the men and women who spread themselves over the earth. Lemuria ends, and the fourth cycle of the Earth incarnation, Atlantis, is about to begin.

In telling the stories of the Old Testament and the Norse Myths, a picture of the evolution of the world and the development of humanity through the Polarean Age to the end of Lemuria is painted.

ATLANTIS

The Old Testament story of Cain and Abel reveals the transition from Lemuria into Atlantis. Again, Cain and Abel do not represent individuals of that time, but rather, they represent humanity at the beginning of Atlantis.

Cain, the first born son of Adam and Eve, is the last born of the Lemurian age and the first born of the Atlantean age. After his birth,

Eve says, "With the help of the Lord I have brought a man into being" (Gen.4:1). This line of Genesis reveals that a divine power is the father of Cain. The curse of the Fall, "and in labour you shall bear children," (Gen.3:16) that was inflicted upon Eve for eating of the forbidden tree, has not yet come into effect, and the hermaphroditic way of birth occurs one last time. Cain's birth is considered a miracle since the new laws of nature have become effective. Abel, the second son of Adam and Eve, is born after the curse has become effective, and he is the first born through the duality of the sexes.[91]

"Man ceased to be merely an organ of the higher divine will streaming through him; self-will was born, and through the activity of new mysterious forces of duality, a chasm opened up between God and Man."[92] Abel carries the heritage of the Fall within him, and as such he knows the difference between good and evil, and he experiences himself as separate from divine existence. Within him grows the desire to reconnect with this divine existence, and in his gift of "some of the first-born of his flock, the fat portions of them" (Gen.4:4) is the first gesture of a religious offering, the beginning of religious history. Cain, on the other hand, is born of Paradise, and the forces of cosmic unity still penetrate him. His name means "the able one," and he still carries within him the developed will forces of the Lemurian age, now in a more human form. The offering he makes, "some of the produce of the soil" (Gen. 4:4), is to a divine spirit who has already withdrawn from the guidance of human evolution, and the divine spirit of the new age does not accept his gift. Abel's gift is appropriately accepted, since he represents humanity of the new age.[93]

As "tiller of the soil" (Gen.4:3), Cain carries within him a capacity that began in the Lemurian age into the new Atlantean age. As such, he represents the development of humanity, and he builds on the future. Man needs to learn to plant, cultivate, and reap, and Cain develops himself to do this work. The future belongs to Cain out of the old creative forces. Even though Abel is a man of the new Atlantean age, as a shepherd, he is not capable of innovation; rather, he is only able to preserve the old.[94] Rudolf Steiner describes the Atlanteans as having a highly developed memory,[95] and this faithful memory did not allow for progress. Rather "one did what one had always 'seen' before. One did not invent; one remembered."[96]

As Cain's heritage is from before the Fall, he is not aware of the difference between good and evil, but as the world begins to absorb the contrast of good and evil, Cain becomes capable of doing good and evil, and "Cain attacked his brother Abel and murdered him" (Gen.

4:8). With this deed self-created harm came into existence, and although Cain is punished for his deed, God ensures that Cain will not be killed for it: for "if anyone kills Cain, Cain shall be avenged sevenfold" (Gen.4:15) showing that the will forces that Cain carries must exist to be utilized and directed for the benefit of humanity. For his punishment, God curses Cain saying, "Now you are accursed, and banished from the ground which has opened its mouth wide to receive your brother's blood, which you have shed. When you till the ground, it will no longer yield you its wealth. You shall be a vagrant and a wanderer on earth" (Gen.4:11-12). To serve the progress of mankind, Cain must take up homelessness, and he must develop new skills to yield from the earth, that which it formerly gave freely.[97]

The Atlanteans were the fourth root race of humankind. The humanity of each of the earth's seven incarnations had characteristics that were quite different from the preceding one. While the Lemurians developed will and imagination, the Atlanteans developed memory and feeling. When a root race begins, its main characteristics are in a youthful state; they slowly mature and then enter a decline. The Atlantean root race can be divided into seven subraces. In his book **Cosmic Memory**, Rudolf Steiner describes the seven subraces of the Atlantean root race.[98] Through the descriptions of these subraces the path of evolution and development can be followed.

The story of Cain and Abel describes the first subrace, where memory and feeling are developed. The development of language is connected with the development of memory, for only after humanity was able to preserve the past was communication through language necessary. The word of the first subrace not only had meaning, but also power, a power that was held to be sacred and was not to be misused.

In the second subrace ambition and a sense of personal value came into being, and it was demanded that deeds be recognized and preserved in memory. The remembrance of ancestors developed. The fifth chapter of **Genesis** gives the record of the descendants of Adam, and in here one can see an echo of the remembrance of ancestors. Social communal life began in the second subrace and was developed in the third, and "the deeds of the ancestors were not to be forgotten by their whole line of descent."[99] However, over the generations, the common consciousness that united descendants with forefathers was gradually lost, and only recent ancestors and not ancient forefathers could be remembered.[100] Personal experience became more important, and along with the remembrance of the past, there was also innovation, and conditions improved. The descendants of Cain can be seen in this description of the third subrace. Jabal "was the ancestor of herdsmen who live in tents" (Gen.4:21), bringing to humanity the art of building houses and breeding animals. Jubul "was the ancestor of those who play the harp and pipe" (Gen.4:21), and Tubal-Cain was "the master of all coppersmiths and blacksmiths" (Gen.4:22), working with the hard mineral kingdom of metals and rocks to bring them into service of life.[101] The third subrace also brought the development of "those who were initiated into the eternal laws of spiritual development."[102] Through a personal ability to develop powers from below, mankind was able to gain enlightenment from above. In this way, the initiates of Atlantis came into being, and "these Initiates became the leaders of the rest of mankind, to whom they were able to communicate the secrets they saw. They trained up disciples, teaching them the paths of attainment of the condition that leads to Initiation. [These Initiates] knew the meaning and purpose of Earth evolution"[103] and could point to the Christ-event as an event coming in the future. The initiates were the teachers of mankind during their first stages of conscious earthly existence.

In the Old Testament, Seth was born to replace Abel (Gen.4:25), and from his descendants Enoch was born, in the seventh generation from Adam. Enoch stands for all of the lofty initiates of Atlantean humanity; with Enoch, human initiates began to guide humanity's destiny. "When Genesis states that Adam remained alive up until the time of Enoch, this is an indication that the primeval wisdom of ancient Lemuria continued to be effective as living inspiration until the initiate wisdom of Atlantis became self-sufficient and found its own mature form."[104]

The few lines of Genesis (5:22-24) that speak of Enoch show that of the descendants from Adam to Noah, he lived the least number of years, but his life span of 365 years represents a complete cycle of time within the Atlantean age. Enoch is also shown special status in that he does not die, but "having walked with God, Enoch was seen no more, because God had taken him away" (Gen.5:24). His ascension into heaven reveals the possibility of victory over death and points to the Christ-event of the future.

In the third subrace of the Atlantean root race, the development of memory led to the development of personal power, and the misuse of this power also arose. In his book *Genesis*, Emil Bock states that legendary tradition reports that Enosh, the son of Seth, was the first idolater and sorcerer, ensouling a human image made of clay with demonic power. The name Enosh means "sick man," and from the beginning, the stream of this "sick man" ran through Atlantean existence.[105]

The misuse of power that flowed from Enosh fully developed in the fourth subrace of the Atlantean root race, using this power to satisfy selfish wishes and desires. Only the faculty of thought could have a restraining effect on such selfish wishes, and this began in the fifth subrace. The faculty of judgment developed, regulating wishes and desires through heeding an inner voice. With the development of the faculty of thought came the loss of control over external natural forces; only the forces of the mineral world, not the life force, could be mastered, a reflection of the descendants of Tubal-cain. A fondness for innovations and changes developed, each person wanting to put into effect what his intelligence suggested to him, bringing about turbulent conditions. The faculty of thought developed further in the sixth subrace, and with it came thought-out laws, the beginning of justice and regulations. The calculating faculty of thought spurred mankind to new enterprises and the beginning of colonization and commerce. The seventh subrace developed thought further, but this population remained faithful to the feeling for memory and the sense that the oldest was the most sensible.

During the Atlantean age, the air was much denser than it is today, and the water was much thinner,[106] and "the earth was completely covered with volumes of watery mist."[107] The physical body of humanity was still soft and pliable, but the events and processes that occurred during the Atlantean evolution brought about the contraction, condensation, and rigidification of Atlantean man; the physical body of man came to maturity in this epoch.[108] In the first half of the Atlantean period, mankind consisted of the physical, etheric, and astral bodies with the ego, which was still wholly outside of mankind. The physical body looked quite different than it does today. The physical body was small in comparison to the gigantic etheric body, creating a clumsy animal-like mass. The bodies of the Atlantean initiates was more similar to the modern form. In those days, thoughts and feelings had a great influence over the physical body, and the initiates were able to mould their bodies until they resembled the modern human form. They did this by placing before their soul the archetype, the spiritual form of modern humanity, a picture, as it were, of what humanity was to become in Post-Atlantean times. Through the power of thoughts and feeling, the initiates of Atlantis brought about the maturity of the physical body.[109] With the turbulence that arose towards the middle of the Atlantean epoch, a great calamity began to gradually overwhelm mankind. "The secrets of the initiates *should* have been carefully protected from those human beings who had not by due preparation purified their astral bodies from error."[110] However, the secrets were shared. This image emerges in Genesis: "when the sons of the gods had intercourse with the daughters of the earth" (Gen.6:4). The secrets were shared with the uninitiated towards an end that was directly opposed to the evolution of mankind, and through the betrayal of the mysteries "a widespread corruption of humanity ensued. The evil grew to greater and greater dimensions."[111]

> When the Lord saw that man had done much evil on earth and that his thoughts and inclinations were always evil, he was sorry that he had made man on earth, and he was grieved at heart. He said, 'This race of men whom I have created, I will wipe them off of the face of the earth - man and beast, reptiles and birds. I am sorry that I ever made them' (Gen.6:5-7).

Thus begins the end of Atlantis.

TRANSITION TO THE POST-ATLANTEAN EPOCH

In the Old Testament stories, the story of Noah and the flood represents the time of transition from the Atlantean to the Post-Atlantean epoch. The flood represents the initiation of a group of people at a

"turning point of evolution by means of the power of the earth's destinies; Noah is the great priestly leader and hierophant in this initiation."[112] Born after Adam and Seth's death, Noah carries a new impulse toward the future. When he is born, Lamech, his father, speaks saying, "This boy will bring us relief from our work, and from the hard labour that has come upon us because of the Lord's curse upon the ground" (Gen.5:29). Before God destroys the world of Atlantis, he tells Noah how to save a portion of creation "to ensure that life continues on earth" (Gen 7:3). When Noah completes God's instructions, the decadence that grew during the Atlantean age takes effect on the watery atmosphere, tremendous storms and hurricanes rise, and rain falls, causing the gradual sinking of Atlantis.[113] "God wiped out every living thing that existed on earth, man and beast, reptile and bird; they were all wiped out over the whole earth, and only Noah and his company in the ark survived" (Gen.7:23). As the separation of earth and water came about at the end of Lemuria, so, too, does a separation of air and water occur at the end of the Atlantean epoch. The dense mists that covered Atlantis scatter, and the sun breaks through. For the first time the blue sky, the sun, moon, and stars are to be seen with the physical eye. As a sign of new life[114] and as a sign of God's covenant that "never again shall all living creatures be destroyed by the waters of a flood, never again shall there be a flood to lay waste the earth" (Gen.9:11), a rainbow appears in the sky.

In Indian mythology, the generations that come after the flood descend from Manu, who is warned of the approaching deluge by a little fish that he finds in his washing water. The fish begs not to be returned to the sea, for it is afraid of the sea monsters. Manu puts the fish in a bowl, but it grows so fast that he has to put it into a jar, then into a lake, and finally back into the sea where it has room to move about. The fish says to Manu, "In seven days there will be the deluge. I shall send a great ship for you and the seven rishis. In it you shall embark a pair of everything that lives upon the earth and in the air, you shall lade it with seeds of every plant, and then you shall go on board. By means of the great serpent Vasuki you shall moor the ship to my horn, and I will guide you over the waters." Manu then becomes the father of the human race.[115] Noah and Manu are one and the same figures.

The story of Job also reflects the transition from Atlantean times to Post-Atlantean times. Job recognizes that there was once a time when humanity was not separated from God, when he was not abandoned by the light of divine wisdom: "if I could only go back to the old days, to the time when God was watching over me, when his lamp shone above my head, and by its light I walked through the darkness" (Job.29:2-3). Divine wisdom can no longer be found (Job 28:12), yet the transition from Atlantean time to Post-Atlantean time is a time when people are able to, of themselves, recognize divine forces which they had hitherto followed unconsciously. This change in awareness is shown in the story of Job. Through his great suffering (Job.1-2), Job is led to the threshold of the spiritual world where he is shown two beasts. On the one side there is a creature whose "tail is rigid as a cedar, the sinews of his flanks are closely knit, his bones are tubes of bronze, and his limbs are like bars of iron" (Job.40:17-18), the hardening Ahrimanic forces. On the other side, there stands the flame of Lucifer; "his sneezing sends out sprays of light, and his eyes gleam like the shimmer of dawn. Firebrands shoot from his mouth, and sparks come streaming out; his nostrils pour forth smoke like a cauldron on a fire blown to full heat. His breath sets burning coals ablaze, and flames flash from his mouth" (Job.41:18-21). This twofold countenance of evil echo the images from the Norse myths of the Fenrir-wolf and Jormungand, the serpent. By the strength that Job gains through his suffering, he is able to behold the sight of these two faces of evil, and they cannot block his way. Job, whose name means 'the tried one, haunted by destiny,' passes the test of suffering and gains entry into the spiritual realm.[116] He can now say, "I knew of thee only by report, but now I see thee with my own eyes" (Job.42:5), and the "Lord restored Job's fortunes and doubled all of his possessions" (Job.42:10).

As the dove that brings the olive branch to Noah represents a spiritual being that hovers over Noah and serves as a prophecy of the dove that appears at the Baptism of Jesus in the Jordan, so does the suffering of Job point to a future event, to the suffering on Golgotha.[117]

Job leads mankind into the future. Post-Atlantean humanity has to deal with the suffering that has come into the world. Through Job it is shown that suffering can be the driving force to inner development; the spiritual fruits of the mystery temples that arise in the Post-Atlantean era are gained when the initiates guide their pupils through suffering and trials so they can become leaders of mankind.[118]

By saving a part of humanity from the flood, Manu-Noah also leads mankind over a threshold. Manu, one of the Initiates from the Atlantean age, is the leader of the Sun-Oracle, or the Christ-Oracle, a mystery centre in Atlantis. His task is to prepare for the future, to train other initiates who would carry humanity forward beyond the time of Atlantis.

The task which the leader imposed upon himself was to bring his followers to the point where, in their own soul, with their own faculty of thought, they could grasp the principles according to which they had hitherto been directed in a way vaguely sensed, but not clearly recognized by them. Men were to recognize the divine forces which they had unconsciously followed. Hitherto, the gods had led men through their messengers; now men were to know about these divine entities. They were to learn to consider themselves as the implementing organs of divine providence.

Now their leader spoke to them in a completely new way. He taught them that invisible powers directed what confronted them visibly, and that they themselves were servants of these invisible powers, that they had to fulfill the laws of these invisible powers with their thoughts. Now they were considered worthy of having the divine messenger speak to them of the gods themselves.[119]

In pointing to the world of divine beings, Manu teaches the first beginnings of thinking. The task of Lemuria was to develop will and imagination; the task of Atlantis was the development of memory and feeling; the task for Post-Atlantean humanity is the development of the faculty of thinking. The power of thought that Manu implanted into the souls of humanity after the flood is the power by which Post-Atlantean mankind is to develop an independent personality and attain freedom.

The great flood of the time of Noah and Manu represents a change of consciousness accompanied by natural disasters. Along with Atlantis, the Atlantean consciousness is washed away by the flood waters. Only those human beings who carry the seed of thought newly implanted by Manu can move forward into a new world with a new consciousness.[120]

OLD INDIAN EPOCH

After the sinking of Atlantis, the fifth cycle of the Earth incarnation begins, the Post-Atlantean cycle. This is the present cycle of the Earth incarnation, and it began with the Old Indian epoch, a time when the Indian civilization was dominant[121] from around 7227 BC until about 5007 BC.[122] The dwellers of ancient India were the descendants of the Atlantean survivors, described in Genesis as "the families of the sons of Noah" (Gen.10:32).

The people of ancient India preserved a clear memory of the Atlantean soul-condition that allowed them to consciously experience

the spiritual world. Only slight preparation was needed to develop the scarcely extinct clairvoyant faculties that allowed the ancient Indians to see into the spiritual world. In fact, the humanity of ancient India believed the spiritual world to be the true, real world, while the sense world, the physical world was only an illusion, maya. They believed the supersensible world to be their true home and strove longingly to return there. There was little interest in what occurred on the physical plane. This resulted in an insufficient penetration of the earthly realm by Old Indian humanity.

Through the work of the seven great teachers, the Old Indian civilization became permeated with supersensible wisdom.[123] In the first Post-Atlantean epoch, a religion developed that recapitulated in spirit what had happened in the first incarnation of the earth when the sun and moon were still bound within the earth. "The spirit who, in the first condition of the earth, in the primeval mist, connected himself with all angels, archangels, high gods and spiritual beings, was for Indian consciousness summed up as a single high individuality under the name of Brahm or Brahma."[124]

Through their clairvoyant faculties, the ancient Indians were able to perceive the fact of repeated earth lives and the laws of karma, knowing that the deeds of life were judged by higher beings after death and would have to be compensated for in subsequent lives. A person's position in life was determined by the previous life.[125] This led to an outstanding feature of old Indian culture - the division of mankind into castes. A soul was not placed randomly into this or that caste, but rather "the seven Holy Rishis who had received their instruction from divine beings in Atlantis could see where each man should be placed."[126]

In teaching the people of old India, the initiates did not speak in words, rather they communicated by supersensible means, passing messages from etheric body to etheric body without the medium of speech. This was possible because the etheric body came to maturity during the Old Indian epoch.[127]

In the Indian story, "The Ramayana,"[128] the demon Ravana appears on the earth and is given power by the Supreme Spirit. The other Gods ask that the creator of the world allow a mortal to be born to kill this demon, the enemy of Gods and sages. Rama, a mortal incarnation of Vishnu, is born to defeat the rakshasa king, Ravana, against whom neither god nor demon can prevail. At the age of 15, Rama is asked to slay two demons. Having done this, he is given another trial; he must bend and string a great bow, a bow that is carried in on an eight-wheeled chariot drawn by 150 men. Rama bends the bow and breaks it in two, winning his wife, Sita. When Rama is chosen to take over the kingdom from his father, King Dasharatha, his stepmother plots against him, and he is banished from his father's kingdom for twice seven years. He is exiled to the forest. Sita, his wife, and Lakshmana, his brother, leave with him. In the forest they observe the vows of ascetics. When Rama's father dies, Bharata, Rama's brother, is chosen to be king. He refuses to be installed as king and seeks Rama, trying to convince him to return to rule the kingdom. Rama refuses, insisting on obeying his father's command, and he bids Bharata to rule "contentedly and righteously." Bharata places a pair of golden sandals before Rama, who steps into them and then out of them. Bharata carries these sandals back to the palace and places them there as symbols of authority while he rules the kingdom from afar. While living in the forest, Rama kills many demons, protecting the ascetics who live there. Towards the end of his time of exile, Sita is stolen by the demon Ravana. With the help of the army of apes, led by Hanuman, Rama goes to rescue her, and in a great battle Rama kills Ravana. Thus the plans of the immortals are fulfilled. After Sita is rescued, Rama refuses to accept her back as his wife, thinking that she is "open to blame." Sita prepares her funeral pyre, but upon entering the flames, Agni, the God of fire, saves her and tells Rama that she is pure and free from sin. Rama accepts her again as his wife. All of the immortals, along with Dasharatha, appear before Rama, and his father speaks saying, "Now I understand how heaven decreed that Ravana should be slain. Now that the immortals have wrought their plan, long may you rule your kingdom with your brothers." Rama is then installed as king, and "the land grew heavy with grain and honey." Rama rules righteously and performs holy sacrifices, and the land is free of evil.

The life of Rama is a continuous struggle against the rakshasas, the demons, of whom he must rid the earth. All of nature, both animal and vegetable, join with Rama in the army of "Good." By always showing correct behaviour and moral goodness, Rama strives to reform morals through teaching by example.[129] Through the trials set before him, Rama is led along the path of initiation to become a leader of ancient India.

The importance of the spiritual world is evident throughout the legends of old India. Sacrifices, meditations, daily rites of worship, and religious rites are performed by the people to bring good and to ward off evil. The small value placed on earthly existence is revealed in the story of "King Shibi"[130] who grants safety to all creatures. A dove, in trying to escape from a hawk, lands in King Shibi's lap. The hawk demands that the king give him the dove to eat as this is his food, and without it he shall die. Not wanting to forsake the dove who came to him for shelter, King Shibi offers an equal amount of flesh from his own body. Cutting off pieces of his flesh and placing them on the opposite side of a scale from the dove, King Shibi must give up his whole body to balance the scales. The Gods then restore King Shibi to life and bestow many blessings upon him. King Shibi values the life of the dove that he was protecting over his own life, and for this he is rewarded by the Gods.

The story of "A Noble Brahman's Sacrifice"[131] also reveals the lack of attachment to earthly existence experienced by the people of old India. In this story, Viravara, a hero, receives five hundred coins from the king each day. Of these coins, two hundred are spent to maintain his household, one hundred are offered to the Gods and two hundred are given away to the Brahmans and poor people. Viravara spends his time in prayer and in guarding the main gate of the palace, not even leaving his post when a shower of arrows rain down on him. From the goddess Earth, Viravara learns that the king is about to die. He asks the goddess if his master's life can be saved through his life or through the life of his wife or children, so that his "birth may be fruitful." Viravara is told that the king's life can be saved if he offers his son as a sacrifice to the goddess Chandika. Viravara tells his wife and son of the goddess's decree, and the boy willingly offers his life as a sacrifice to the goddess on the king's behalf. Viravara chops off his son's head "for indeed those who are devoted to the welfare of their masters take no delight in their own lives or those of their sons." Upon the death of his son, Viravara's daughter and wife also die. He, being alone now, decides to take his own life, but is stopped from doing so by a voice from heaven. In return for the integrity that he has shown, Viravara is offered a blessing and is granted the lives of his wife and children again and long life for the king. Viravara makes no mention of these events to the king, but, unbeknown to him, the king has witnessed all that has taken place. He rewards Viravara, who, with his family, then lives in contentment.

Many stories reveal the use of clairvoyant communication, particularly the story of "Blind Man, Deaf Man and Donkey,"[132] where the deaf man talks with the blind man. This can happen only if their communication is not dependent on audible speech.

OLD PERSIAN EPOCH

Long did the Indian culture endure, and following it there came the second epoch of Post-Atlantean evolution, Old Persian, when the civilization of ancient Persia was dominant, reaching a culmination in Zarathustra. The Old Persian epoch began around 5067 BC and lasted until about 2907 BC.[133] The people of this epoch had a different task from the people of the Old Indian epoch. While the people of old India longed for the spiritual world, the people of ancient Persia became more suited to the physical world of the senses. They learned to love the earth and what could be gained from it.[134] The physical world became the field of work. The people changed from being hunters and gatherers and became land dwellers, settling the earth and building cities. The substitution of agriculture for nomadic food gathering was the result of a change of consciousness that took place during the Old Persian epoch and a result of a new orientation towards the earth, a new relationship with the earth. The people of old Persia saw the earth as their home.[135]

During the second Post-Atlantean epoch, mankind incarnated further into the physical body. The ancient faculty of clairvoyance existed, because the etheric body of mankind was somewhat independent of the physical body and extended beyond it. During the Old Persian epoch, the etheric body began to shrink and adjusted itself to the form of the physical body. The physical and etheric bodies grew closer together, and the faculty of clairvoyance began to die out.[136] The astral body of mankind came to maturity, and with this new maturity came the possibility of doing evil. For the first time the forces of Ahriman, the lord of evil and illusion, began to work in the astral body of mankind. Ahriman attained dominion on the earth with the betrayal of the secrets of the initiates.[137] Ahriman's task was to hinder the development of mankind, to tempt mankind into believing that they were solely beings of the earth, to have them forget their divine origins and the mission set them by the Gods.[138] Ahriman tempted humans to become deeply involved in the earth, to enter into the darkness of the earth. As a result of this Ahrimanic activity, mankind lost sight of the spiritual worlds, and the people of old Persia no longer knew themselves as spiritual beings. The people experienced a sense of being abandoned by the Gods, and they began to fear death. The search for immortality began.

The people of old Persia were in danger of developing such a strong attachment to the physical world that it became possible for their souls to lose all connection with the supersensible world. A strong spiritual impulse was needed to counteract these qualities in their character. The leader assigned to the ancient Persian culture by the Guardian of the Sun Oracle was Zarathustra.[139] His task was to reveal the secrets that he received from Ahura Mazda, the Wise Lord, the Lord of the Sun. Zarathustra was to show the people the dangers that they were exposed to by Ahriman, the destructive spirit. He showed the people that the sense world was not void of spirit. This polarity of forces of good and evil battled against each other, and their battleground was the soul of mankind.[140] In the religious consciousness of the Old Persian epoch, the principles of light and darkness existed, personified in Ahura Mazda and Ahriman. This was a remembrance of the time when the sun left the earth, thereby forming the duality of earth evolution.[141]

Towards the end of the Old Persian epoch the direct perception of the spiritual world was almost wholly extinct, and the Kali Yuga, the Dark Age, began lasting until the turn of the twentieth century AD.[142]

The clairvoyant consciousness ended, and humanity could no longer communicate as they did throughout the Old Indian epoch, by means of passing messages from etheric body to etheric body. In striving to regain the spiritual world that was lost, mankind began to build towers, a materialistic way of striving towards heaven.

The images of this time are revealed in the Old Testament story of the Tower of Babel (Gen.11:1-9). At a time when all the world speaks a single language, the people decide to make bricks and bake them hard. With these bricks they make a city and a "tower with its top in the heavens" so that they can make a name for themselves. When the Lord sees this he decides to "confuse their speech, so that they will not understand what they say to one another." "The last remnant of God's Word, which united human beings, is silenced in human language. No longer does speech come from above, there is only speaking from below. As speech becomes devoid of God, it splits up into the many languages that have no linking bridge between them, men no longer understand each other."[143] The people leave off building the city, and it is known as Babel for there the Lord "made a babble of the language of all the world," and "men scattered all over the face of the earth"; the age of the isolated nations that fight against each other begins.

In the creation myth of ancient Persia, Ahura Mazda dwells in endless light, and in the deepest darkness dwells the evil Ahriman. They have no contact with each other for they are separated by "the void." They both exist without coming into contact with each other. Ahura Mazda knows of the existence of Ahriman; Ahriman does not know that Ahura Mazda exists, but when he sees his light, he is prompted to attack and destroy. Ahura Mazda offers Ahriman peace, which he rejects, but he does agree to battle for a fixed period of time. Then comes a time where there exists a mixing of the wills of good and evil. This will be followed by a time when the evil spirit will be defeated.[144]

By transforming the earth, by becoming beings capable of working upon the earth, the people of Old Persia felt that they could unite with the good Gods and vanquish Ahriman, the evil god in matter. "They hoped that the earth would become a good planet one day, that it would be redeemed and that a glorification of Ahura Mazda, the highest being would come about."[145]

The myth of Ahura Mazda and Ahriman shows that there was a time when the Ahrimanic forces did not influence mankind, but since the "mixing of the wills of good and evil," the battle between the two continues. In Persian mythology, this struggle continues even after death, for "even after death, for the first three days and nights, demons lie in wait to attack the soul, especially that of a virtuous man."[146] These three nights are "a time of regret for the soul, regret at the death of the body, and a time of yearning for reunification of the body with the soul."[147] This picture greatly contrasts that of the Old Indian epoch.

During the three days after death, the soul is protected by the prayers and offerings of the deceased's relatives who must not bewail their loss too much for their tears form a barrier for the soul on its journey into the afterlife. After three days have passed, the soul is judged; the store of merits and faults are weighed in the balances before the eyes of three judges. If the good thoughts, words, and actions outweigh the evil ones, the soul is guided by a beautiful maiden and a fragrant wind across the broad Chinvat bridge to heaven. If evil outweighs good, then an old hag and a foul smell lead the wicked soul, chased by its evil deeds in the form of a wild beast, to the Chinvat bridge, which is turned to present a sharp edge, like a sword. From there the soul falls into the abyss of hell where it is subjected to corrective punishment that matches its sins. Hell is not eternal, and it prepares all souls to participate in the final resurrection. If the good and bad deeds balance each other, the soul proceeds to an intermediate place.[148] Such a story reveals the fear of death experienced by mankind in old Persia.

Of the beneficent animals of Persian mythology, there are ten fishes who ceaselessly guard the Gaokernea tree from the attacks of an evil lizard. From the fruit of this tree comes the elixir of immortal life.[149] Immortality is a quest that becomes important for humanity towards the end of the Old Persian epoch.

THE EPIC OF GILGAMESH

With the onset of the Kali Yuga, the ancient clairvoyant faculty was extinguished in human souls, and darkness surrounded mankind. The gaze of humanity was turned from the spiritual world to the physical world. This was a turning point in the evolution of consciousness, and along with the faculty of thought, the sense organs developed and became capable of distinct sense perceptions, which increasingly replaced the remains of ancient clairvoyance. Through the senses, mankind received the abundance that the physical world had to offer. This caused a faintness of consciousness for mankind, and an oppressive condition of sleep came over the people. The soul of humanity acquired a first point of ego,[150] and with the increased self-consciousness there also came a greater awareness of death, a sorrowful event that cut humanity off from the fullness of life on earth. Thus, the search for immortality became important.

Gilgamesh, a figure from mythological history, represents in picture-form what is happening in the souls of mankind as humanity moves from the Old Persian epoch into the Egypto/Chaldean epoch. He portrays the end of a certain soul condition taking place in humanity and the beginning of a new soul condition, the sentient soul.

Gilgamesh[151] is a builder of walls. He builds a wall around the city of Uruk, separating the city from "nature," from the abundance of the physical world. The people of Uruk complain to the Gods about Gilgamesh's arrogance and tyranny, and in answer to their prayers, "noble Enkidu" is created. Innocent of mankind, he lives in the wilderness, living with the animals. The people of the country complain to Gilgamesh about this wildman, and he sends a woman from the temple of love to tame him. After Enkidu has lain with her "for six days and seven nights," he tries to return to the animals, but they run from him. He is not able to follow for his swiftness is gone and he has "grown weak, for wisdom was in him, and the thoughts of a man were in his heart." So he returns to the woman, and she begins to civilize him, clothing him and bringing him to the shepherds where he learns to eat bread, for "it is the staff of life" and drink wine for "it is the custom of the land." Having become a man, Enkidu is brought to the city where he cries aloud, "I have come to change the old order." Enkidu and Gilgamesh wrestle in the streets of Uruk until Enkidu is thrown, whereupon they embrace, and their friendship is sealed.

According to Rudolf Steiner, Enkidu, as the wildman, is clairvoyant, but this faculty is lost when he becomes entangled with the earthly plane through the woman.[152] In the city, Enkidu becomes the catalyst for changing the old order.

Enkidu becomes oppressed by the idleness of the city, and Gilgamesh feels he has not yet fulfilled the decree of his destiny and so Gilgamesh decides to go into the "Country of the Living" to destroy the evil in the land. Through this great deed he hopes to make a name for himself, a name "stamped on brick," a name that will endure, thereby gaining a form of immortality; he knows that "only the gods live for ever" while the days of men are numbered.

Enkidu changes the order of things by leading the men of the city into the "Country of the Living," the country of the life forces, a fluid world of dreams. Together they go into the forest, and they come to the green mountain. There they stand still, struck dumb, gazing at the forest. Gilgamesh seizes his axe and fells one of the trees of the Cedar Forest. Humbaba, the guardian of the forest, cries out, and when faced with the protector of the natural world, Gilgamesh is seized by sleep and lays on the ground sleeping deeply. His consciousness is not able to confront the physical world, the world of the senses.

Humbaba, being granted "sevenfold terrors," was placed by the Gods to protect the Cedar Forest. He never sleeps, and he knows every part of this realm. He can hear a wild heifer stir "in the forest, though she is sixty leagues" away. Here there is a reflection of Heimdall who guards Bifrost through the "knowingness" of the Lemurian age. Perhaps it is this faculty from a time now past that makes Humbaba evil.

Humbaba puts on the first of his seven splendours, and Gilgamesh and Enkidu quickly set out to trap him before he can put on the remaining six – for if he clothes himself in his seven splendours, they will have no chance of capturing him. Gilgamesh cries out to Shamash, who summons the eight winds to rise up against Humbaba; they rise up and he is "gripped, unable to go forward or back." Then Gilgamesh and Enkidu cut seven cedars, and "seven times Humbaba loosed his glory on them." Tears come into Humbaba's eyes, and he asks to be set free, trying to make a bargain with Gilgamesh. Gilgamesh's heart is moved by compassion, and he wishes to set Humbaba free, but Enkidu insists that "Humbaba must die." On the third blow Humbaba falls, and his seven splendours are given away to nature. The Gods are angry that Humbaba has been killed.

After the battle with Humbaba, Gilgamesh is wooed by Ishtar, the goddess of love, but he rejects her love, knowing that she destroys her lovers, changing them into animals. In her anger, she asks her father for the Bull of Heaven, seven years drought, to destroy Gilgamesh, threatening to break open the doors of hell if he does not grant her request. Gilgamesh and Enkidu kill the Bull of Heaven, offer the heart to Shamash and throw the thigh to Ishtar.

The bull represents the ancient blood rites and the clairvoyant consciousness that was maintained by the blood of the tribe. Individual consciousness moves away from the tribal or group consciousness. The Bull is also the symbol of the approaching epoch, the time of Taurus.

The Gods take counsel, and because Gilgamesh and Enkidu have killed Humbaba and the Bull of Heaven, one of the two must die. Enkidu is struck with mortal sickness. As he lies on his sick bed, he dreams, learning "that misery comes at last to the healthy man, the end of life is sorrow." After twelve days of suffering, Enkidu dies, not a hero's death, but ingloriously by disease. For seven days and seven nights Gilgamesh laments for Enkidu. Despair fills his heart, and he becomes afraid of death. He seeks Utnapishtim, the one mortal who has been granted everlasting life by the Gods, so that he can "question him concerning the living and the dead." Gilgamesh goes in search of the secret of immortality. He travels for twelve leagues in darkness through the mountain to the garden of the Gods. There he meets Siduri, the maker of wine. She tells him that he will never find what he is seeking, for the Gods have allotted death to mankind, keeping eternal life for themselves. Therefore, he should give up his quest, and fill his belly with good things, dance, be merry, feast, and rejoice – to enjoy the abundance of the physical world. He refuses to give up his quest, and she directs him to the ferryman, Urshanabi, who will ferry him across the Ocean to Utnapishtim. In order to cross the Ocean, Gilgamesh has to cut and pitch one hundred and twenty poles and place them in the boat. He and Urshanabi set off for Utnapishtim. When they come to the waters of death, Gilgamesh uses the poles to push the boat across the water. All of the poles are used before they reach the opposite shore, so Gilgamesh removes his clothing, and, using them as a sail and himself as a mast, they are carried across the waters of death. Dressed in the skins of animals, Gilgamesh approaches Utnapishtim who tells him that there is no permanence to life; however, he is willing to test Gilgamesh. Gilgamesh must "only prevail against sleep for six days and seven nights." Of all of his ordeals, this is the only one that Gilgamesh is unable to triumph over, and he falls asleep. Utnapishtim's wife bakes a loaf of bread for every day that Gilgamesh sleeps. When he awakens, he sees the loaves of bread and knows that he has failed; he will not find the answer he seeks, and wherever his foot rests, there he finds death.

Utnapishtim banishes Urshanabi, who then remains with Gilgamesh. Gilgamesh removes his animal skins and dresses in clothes given to him by Utnapishtim that will show no sign of age and will alway wear like new garments, until his journey is ended and he reaches his city once more. Even though Gilgamesh fails his test, Utnapishtim, at the request of his wife, reveals to him the secret of the plant of rejuvenation, a plant that grows under water and has a prickle like a thorn. If he is able to get this plant, then he will hold that which restores lost youth. Tying stones to his feet, Gilgamesh sinks to the water bed where he grasps the plant. Cutting the stones from his feet, he returns to shore. He calls the plant "The Old Men Are Young Again" and plans on taking it to the old men of Uruk. On the way home, Gilgamesh stops to bathe at a well, but deep in the pool there is a serpent. The serpent senses the sweetness of the flower and snatches it away. Immediately it sheds its skin. The snake gains the power to be born anew, and in despair Gilgamesh returns home, where he engraves the whole story on a stone.

Gilgamesh does not succeed at the task that he himself chooses to undertake, the destiny he sets for himself. The destiny that is decreed for him by the Gods, however, is fulfilled. Kingship is his destiny; everlasting life is not.

EGYPTO/CHALDEAN EPOCH

While Gilgamesh searched for immortality, Hermes taught humanity "how in the body-free condition after death man would be living in the world of Spirit-beings."[153] Hermes Trismegistos was the guiding spirit of civilization in the third Post- Atlantean epoch, which evolved among the Chaldeans, Babylonians, Assyrians, and Egyptians, an epoch referred to by Steiner as the Egypto/Chaldean epoch. Hermes first showed mankind the "entire physical world as the handwriting of the gods. ... He gave ... what had to be deciphered as the deed of the gods in the physical world."[154]

The supersensible faculties that were available to humanity in earlier epochs were now mostly lost, and mankind could no longer see into the spiritual worlds. Instead, the people of the Egypto/Chaldean epoch had to search in the physical world for manifestations of the spiritual world, to find the Spirit-beings through their counterparts in the physical and sense-perceptible realm. Mankind had to look towards the physical world to see in it the laws and workings of the Spirit-World.[155]

The Egyptian had confidence in the laws that man could find in the physical world, through which man can master matter. By this means arose geometry, mathematics. With the help of this, man could rule the elements because he trusted in what his spirit could find, because he believed that he could imprint the spirit upon matter. Thus he could build the pyramids, the temples, and the sphinxes. This was a mighty step in the conquest of the physical plane that was accomplished in the third cultural period. Man had progressed so far that for the first time he was able rightly to respect the physical plane. The physical world began to mean something to him.[156]

Hermes taught that in as much as humanity worked in accordance with the aims of the Spirit Powers, so they would prepare themselves to be united with these Powers after death.[157]

The "Egyptians considered the heart to be the seat of the mind or intelligence,"[158] and they interpreted the world through their feelings. They were not yet capable of intellectual thinking. As a result of this, the ancient Egyptians saw no contradiction in the various stories of creation.[159] It did not matter if creation flowed from Ra and his succeeding generations, from Ptah, through frogs and serpents, by Geb the goose that laid the cosmic egg, or through the creator-god, Amon.[160] Instead of one cult trying to suppress the others, Egyptian civilization was syncretic, combining the different beliefs and thereby enriching the whole.

OSIRIS - ISIS

The beginning of the sentient soul age, the third Post - Atlantean epoch, can be explored through the Osiris - Isis myth.[161] When Osiris is born, a voice from out of the heavens proclaims: "Now has come the lord of all things," and a good and wise king appears among men. Men are savages when Osiris first comes among them; they hunt wild animals and wander in broken tribes fighting fiercely amongst each other. Evil are their ways, and their desires are sinful. Such is the condition of mankind at the beginning of the Dark Age. Osiris ushers in a new age. He makes good and binding laws, he utters just decrees, and he judges with wisdom between men. He teaches men how to plant seeds, reap the harvest, grind the corn, and knead the flour and meal, so that they may have food in plenty. He trains vines and cultivates fruit trees, causing the fruit to be gathered. Osiris teaches the people to worship the Gods and to live holy lives. The hand of man is no longer lifted against his brother, and there is peace and prosperity in the land. Seeing the good work that he has accomplished in Egypt, Osiris travels the world teaching wisdom to mankind and prevailing upon them to give up their evil ways. He achieves his triumphs by gentle and persuasive speech, by music and song, not by battle conquest. Peace follows him, and men learn wisdom from him. Such is the new age issued in by Osiris.

Through Osiris, the people of the Egypto/Chaldean era develop a feeling for the physical world that is different from that experienced by the ancient Persians. By living into and working upon the world of the senses, using their own human faculties, the conquest of the physical world can come about, which must be regarded as the mission of Post-Atlantean mankind. By discovering and inventing the means of civilization and what this world provides, mankind is able to continue the development of soul.[162] The great inventions of the sentient soul epoch come at the beginning of this period, inspired by higher beings who are working at the task of preparing mankind for future life on earth.[163]

While Osiris is away from Egypt, Isis, his sister and wife, rules over the land. Set (Typhon), Osiris's brother, regards with jealous eyes the good work of his brother, and he seeks to stir up rebellion in the land, for he loves warfare better than peace. Isis frustrates his wicked desires, and Set grows angry. When Osiris returns to Egypt, there is great rejoicing and feasting. To the merrymaking Set and his conspirators bring a shapely and decorated chest, which is made to the exact measurements of Osiris's body. He then proclaims that he will make a gift of the chest to whoever's body fits its proportions exactly. No one suspects any evil, and all the guests try the chest, but no one can win it. Then Osiris comes forward; "he lay down within the chest, and he filled it in every part." Set and his followers immediately spring up, shut the lid, nail it fast, and solder it with lead. Set commands his followers to carry the chest away, and they hasten away with it and throw it into the Nile, where it is carried out to sea. So ends Osiris's reign upon the land of Egypt.

When Isis hears what has happened, she cries bitterly and wanders up and down the land seeking the body of Osiris. Seven scorpions follow and protect her. While she searches for the body, Set ascends the throne of Osiris and reigns over Egypt. Tyranny and great disorder prevail, and people are persecuted.

The coffin of Osiris is carried by the sea to Byblos, in Syria (Phoenicia), where it is cast onto the shore. A sacred tree springs up and grows around it, the body of Osiris enclosed in its great trunk. The King of the land marvels at this tree, because of its rapid growth, and has it cut down to be erected in his house as a sacred pillar. A revelation comes to Isis, and she sets out for Byblos where she finds favour in the eyes of the queen. She is chosen to be the foster-mother for the queen's child. At night she takes the child and holds it in a fire to burn away its mortality. One night the queen sees her child in the flames and immediately snatches him away, denying him immortality. Isis reveals who she is and asks the king for the sacred pillar. She cuts deep within its trunk and removes the chest that has been concealed there, taking it back to Egypt, hiding it in a secret place.

While mourning over Osiris's body, Isis conceives a son, but before he is born, Set discovers the body of Osiris hidden in the Delta marsh reeds. Set cuts the body into fourteen pieces and throws them into the Nile for the crocodiles to eat. These creatures do not touch them, and the pieces are scattered along the river banks. Isis searches for the fragments of her husband's body and recovers all of them except one piece that has been eaten by a fish. By the rites of embalming, Isis brings Osiris back to life, but he does not wish to remain in the land of the living, preferring eternal life as king of the dead. To this land he returns, becoming the Judge of the dead.

Horus, the son of Isis and Osiris, grows to manhood. One night Osiris appears to him in a dream, urging him to overthrow Set. Horus vows to drive his wicked uncle out of Egypt and goes forth to battle. Many battles follow, and the last battle is fought for many days. Horus loses an eye, and Set is grievously wounded and driven out of the kingdom. The god Thoth descends from heaven and heals the wounds of both men. Set tries to claim the throne, but the Gods judge Horus to be the rightful king. Horus re-establishes the reign of justice and is the model for all the following pharaohs, who each take the title "Living Horus." The trinity that came about in the earth's evolution with the separation of the moon in the Lemurian cycle is exemplified in Osiris, Isis, and Horus.[164]

Osiris is killed by his brother Typhon, the god of wind. This myth reveals a great cosmic event, the separation of the light and air that occurred on Old Moon; the first breathing of the air-breath that brought the first awareness of death to mankind murders Osiris. "The Egyptian experienced the god who came from the sun and was still in harmony with his brother as Osiris. Typhon was the air-breath that had brought mortality to man. Here we see one of the most pregnant examples of how the facts of cosmic evolution repeat themselves in man's inner knowledge."[165]

The forces of the human soul are still directed to the supersensible world, but can no longer develop the faculties of the soul. The ancient clairvoyant forces are now amidst the dead, and Osiris is the Judge of the dead. Imaginative clairvoyance disappears from the earth as a normal faculty of the human soul. The seven scorpions that follow Isis indicate that the old clairvoyant forces left the earth when the sun was in Scorpio,[166] thus indicating the first beginnings of astrology that arise in the Egypto/Chaldean epoch.

Steiner interprets Typhon's placing Osiris in a chest and casting it into the sea as an event that corresponds with the separation of the moon; Osiris withdraws with the moon and is in cosmic space. When he is found again, he is in fourteen pieces. "The fourteen aspects of the moon [from new to full moon] are the fourteen pieces of the dismembered Osiris. The complete Osiris is the whole moon-disk."[167] The fourteen phases from full moon to new moon are in turn ruled by Isis.

The Egypto/Chaldean epoch furnishes a mirroring knowledge and experience of what happened in the Lemurian time, of what happened on earth during and after the departure of the moon.[168]

The Osiris-Isis myth also indicates the disappearance of the ancient picture-script and the beginning of the abstract script, a script that no longer expresses mysteries but only serves to express the sense world. The letter script originated in Phoenicia, where Isis goes to find the body of Osiris. This means "to find the picture-script transformed into the letter- script,"[169] which is then brought back to Egypt.

ABRAHAM - ISAAC

During the third Post-Atlantean epoch, humanity did not yet act independently as fully self-conscious beings, for the "I" was not yet incorporated within mankind. Action came from the inspiration of higher beings. Inspirations were received through dreams, which at first the people could interpret for themselves, but later they lost the ability to do so. Clairvoyance could be acquired through initiation into the mysteries, and as well, the people learned to discover the will of the Gods by observing the heavens, through astrology. Monotheism appeared for the first time in history toward the end of the sentient soul age.[170] Akhenaton believed in the "one and only god," Aton, and in his early reign he waged a war of bitter persecution against Amon, chipping away the God's name from every monument. It was at this time that he officially changed his name to "Akhen-aton" (formerly Amenhotep IV), meaning "the spirit of Aton." He ascended the throne with the noble desire to make mankind wise, just, free, and mild. He thought it sinful to shed blood or to take life away and would not send troops to help in the battles of the country. Only the fruits of the earth were laid on the altars of his temples, and no sacrifices were offered there. He felt Aton was revealed in beauty, and his worshippers had to lead beautiful lives. No statues of Aton were made, for Akhenaton forbade idolatrous customs.[171] Akenaton tried to introduce a monotheistic state religion, but he was ahead of his time. The people of the sentient soul age could not yet accept monotheism, and Akhenaton's religion did not survive after his death.

The sentient soul age was described earlier as being a time when humanity had to seek the presence of the spiritual world in the physical world. In Abraham, the thinking spirit awakens, guiding his senses and allowing him to perceive "the Creator in the multiplicity of creations."[172] He was able to perceive the one divine ego, and through him humanity began to seek the one divinity, the one Creator of all creatures.

The Genesis story of Abraham begins with the Lord telling him to leave his country and to go to a new country that will be shown to him (Gen.12:1). His mission does not lie within the old, but rather, something new is to proceed from him. Abram, as he is yet called, travels with Sarai, his wife, and Lot, his nephew, to the new country, where he builds an altar to the Lord and invokes the Lord by name (Gen.12:8), the first human to do so. Yet, Abram does not remain in this new land. He travels to Egypt (Gen.12:10) and there encounters the Egyptian pyramids, structures that were built with forces common to pre-Atlantis, the forces of the etheric body that had not yet been incorporated into the physical body and which made physical accomplishments feasible. These structures are quite different from the brick structures that Abram is familiar with in his homeland; Abram is touched by a spirit differing from that of his homeland. In Egypt, Abram enters into the world of the still genuine death mysteries. He absorbs into his being what the Egyptian mysteries can give him to help him fulfill his mission.[173] His mission cannot be fulfilled in Egypt, and through various stages he returns to "where he had set up an altar on the first occasion and had invoked the Lord by name" (Gen.13:4), carrying within him something of the cultures from the two lands he had left behind into the land of his own destiny.[174] Lot and Abram part company (Gen.12:12).

After the battle with the kings (Gen.12:12-17), Abram meets Melchizedek and gives "him a tithe of all the booty" (Gen.12:20). Melchizedek is none other than Manu, the leader of the Atlantean sun mysteries, who through the milennia has guided the spiritual destinies of Post-Atlantean humanity, and who works through Zarathustra and Hermes, his disciples. Now Abram, as did Gilgamesh, learns from Noah, becoming a disciple and messenger of Noah.[175] "Abraham encountered not a man but a world. He came to a mystery centre whose guiding spirit was Melchizedek and through Melchizedek to the great Manu himself, and he gained a decisive share of the mysteries alive there."[176] In order to partake in these holy mysteries, Abram gives Melchizedek one-tenth of what he has. Sarai has not borne Abram any children, so she gives him her slave girl, Hagar, hoping to have a family through her. Abram lays with Hagar and conceives a son who is to be called Ishmael. God made "of him a great nation" (Gen.20:19). His descendents lead to Mohammed, and the Islamic religion.[177]

When Abram is ninety-nine, the Lord appears to him and makes a covenant with him. He promises to be his God and the God of his descendants (Gen.17:8). Abram seals this covenant with the introduction of the rite of circumcision (Gen.17:11). The Lord changes Abram's name to "Abraham" (Gen.17:5), "Father of nations," and he changes Sarai's name to "Sarah" (Gen.17:15). As once God "breathed his divine breath into Adam, now with the 'H' sound, he breathes into the 'name' of man a hint of the future,"[178] a sign that the convenant signifies a kind of new creation of mankind. The generations following from Abraham are for the purpose of building a form, a vessel for the divine spirit. "The preparation of a body capable of receiving the Christ spirit [is] a part of the Hebrew mission"[179] and to prepare the way for the full incarnation of the human "I."

When God tells Abraham that Him alone must they worship, he prepares mankind for the coming of the self-conscious ego. In order for monotheism to be accepted, the sentient soul of mankind has to undergo a change. For a personal relationship to exist between God and man, a change in consciousness has to happen.[180] This is the transition from the sentient soul age to the intellectual soul age. When God changes Sarah's name, he also promises Abraham a son by her, who is to be called Isaac. Abraham laughs, for he is one-hundred, and Sarah is ninety, and he wonders how they can have a son, but God says: "My covenant I will fulfil with Isaac, whom Sarah will bear to you at this season next year" (Gen17:21). The Lord makes good his promise; Sarah and Abraham have a son, but then the Lord demands Abraham to sacrifice this son (Gen 22:2). Abraham takes his son, wood for the fire, and a knife, and goes to the place God has appointed for the sacrifice. Isaac questions his father, "where is the young beast for the sacrifice" (Gen.22:8). Abraham tells him that God will provide the beast. "Abraham built an altar and arranged the wood. He bound his son Isaac and laid him on the altar on top of the wood. Then he stretched out his hand and took the knife to kill his son" (Gen.22:9-11). He is stopped by the angel of the Lord. Abraham passes the test that God has set him. Abraham "saw a ram caught by its horns in a thicket. So he went and took the ram and offered it as a sacrifice instead of his son" (Gen.22:13). Not only is Abraham tested but Isaac also; he undergoes the "initiation death that leads to resurrection."[181] In the "ram" Abraham and Isaac see the sun in the sign of Aries at a time when the sun is still in the sign of Taurus. A vision of the future is shown, a vision of when the sun faculties of Isaac's nature will be fulfilled. These faculties have to be "sacrificed" in the present for the sake of the future.[182] The sacrifice of Isaac, the sacrifice of a son, is also a precursor to the sacrifice of the Son of God and a reflection of the death of Baldur.

Akhenaton is ahead of his time, but Abraham is the personification of a stream of humanity that has adjusted to a new world condition.

The end of the sentient soul age is marked by the end of polytheism and the emergence of monotheism.

> Abraham's perception of God was a specific one. It was the fruit of a special transformation of the human organism and consciousness, which Abraham, blazing the trail for all mankind, experienced for the first time. By virtue of the now clearly sculptured instrument of the brain, the human spirit in Abraham became capable of perceiving the world of the spirit ruling therein through mirror images of thought. In this manner he also confronted the divine unity, which his thinking sought and found in the multitude of phenomena.[183]

In this way Abraham points towards the future.

TRANSITION TO INTELLECTUAL SOUL AGE: JACOB - JOSEPH

Isaac marries Rebecca. She conceives, and the Lord tells her that she carries two nations in her womb, "one shall be stronger than the other; the older shall be servant to the younger" (Gen.25:23). From Isaac and Rebecca, Jacob and Esau are born, Jacob the younger and Esau the older. Jacob becomes the third in the trinity of patriarchs: Abraham the root of Israel's life; Isaac the root of its spirit; and Jacob the root of its soul.[184] Jacob's destiny is one of struggle; even in the womb he struggles. At birth Esau "the first came out red, hairy all over like a hair-cloak" (Gen. 25:25), and "immediately afterwards his brother was born with his hand grasping Esau's heel" (Gen.25:26).

Although Jacob is born later, he carries faculties of progress and of the future. Esau belongs to an ancient world order as shown in the words: "Esau became skillful in hunting" (Gen.25:27). His heel is weak from being grasped by Jacob, and he cannot move forward, but can only limp behind.[185] Esau, "the hairy one," can be regarded as a wildman, not unlike Enkidu before he is tamed. When Adam and Eve leave Paradise, God makes them "tunics of skins" (Gen.3:21), and when Gilgamesh went to visit Utnapishtim, he wore clothes of animal skins. These hairy skins are symbols of the ancient etheric forces.[186]

Jacob is the image of intellectual cleverness, a picture of the evolution of mankind moving from the sentient soul age to the intellectual soul age. Through cunning Jacob gains the advantage over Esau. One day Jacob makes a broth, and when Esau comes in from hunting, he asks for some. Jacob will not give him any unless he sells him his birthright, the right of the first born. Esau agrees (Gen.25:29-34), showing how little he values his birthright.

Passing on the birthright to the first born is an inheritance that preserves the forces of the past unchanged. With each generation, however, spiritual progress has to be attained, and so the dominance of the natural laws has to be eliminated somewhat. "Only an inheritance that became spiritualized was suitable for preparing the way and the vessel for the future of God."[187] Jacob is the first one to consciously break the natural law, but he also has to suffer the consequences that result from eliminating the old order. By taking hold of the intellect, Jacob makes a bold step forward.

When Isaac grows old, he becomes blind. Before he dies, he wishes to give his blessing to Esau, so he asks him to prepare a "savoury dish" so that he can bestow his blessings on him. Rebecca hears this, and she tells Jacob to prepare a dish and bring it to his father, so that he can receive his father's blessing instead. Rebecca takes Esau's clothes and puts them on Jacob, covering his hands and neck with goatskin, so that should Isaac touch him, he will think that he is touching Esau. Jacob goes to Isaac and offers him the food, and Isaac, not knowing it is Jacob in front of him, gives him his blessing. For the second time Jacob gets what rightfully belongs to Esau. Esau holds a grudge against Jacob and threatens to kill him after Isaac has died. Rebecca hears this and sends Jacob away (Gen.27). While Jacob journeys to the land of his forefathers, he comes to a certain place and rests there for the night, using a stone for his pillow. While he sleeps, he dreams:

> He dreamt that he saw a ladder, which rested on the ground with its top reaching to heaven, and angels of God were going up and down upon it. The Lord was standing beside him and said, 'I am the Lord, the God of your father Abraham and the God of Isaac. This land on which you are lying I will give to you and your descendants. They shall be countless as the dust upon the earth, and you shall spread far and wide, to north and south, to east and west. All the families of the earth shall pray to be blessed as you and your descendants are blessed. I will be with you, and I will not leave you until I have done all that I have promised.' ... Thereupon Jacob made this vow: 'If God will be with me, if he will protect me on my journey and give me food to eat and clothes to wear, and I come

back safely to my father's house, then the Lord shall be my God.' (Gen.28:12f)

Jacob, the human being who becomes intellectual and separated from the supersensible world, is blessed with a spiritual experience; he is received back into the fullness of spiritual existence, experiencing himself in the spiritual world at night time.[188]

Jacob comes to the home of his kinsman, who has two daughters, Leah, the older one, and Rachel, the younger one. He falls in love with Rachel and agrees to work for seven years to gain her as his wife, but at the end of the seven years he is given Leah instead, for it is not right to give the younger sister in marriage before the elder sister. Jacob works for another seven years, gains Rachel as his wife, and then works for a final seven years (Gen.29:1-30). Jacob again tries to bypass the old world order but here, in the old world, the rights of the first born must be recognized. Leah is an image of the inherited soul forces, while Rachel, which means "the ram's lamb," is a manifestation of the spiritual forces of the future.[189]

Jacob works for his kinsman, and using his cleverness once again, he gains wealth and increases his flocks (Gen.30:32-43). Then with his sons and his wives, his herds and his livestock, he sets off to return to Isaac. On the journey he is met by the angels of God (Gen.32:2), a daytime reflection of what he had experienced in the night time at the beginning of his journey. Later, Jacob has another dream of fighting with a man, an angel, all night. At daybreak the man asks to be let go, but Jacob refuses to do so unless the man blesses him first. The man blesses him and changes his name to Israel, because he "strove with God and with men and prevailed" (Gen.32:28).

This is Jacob's third and most significant spiritual experience. He had gained his father's blessing through cleverness, but here he gains a divine blessing by courage of soul and inner strength. He leaves saying, "I have seen God face to face and my life is spared" (Gen.32:31). The sun rises when Jacob leaves, indicating that "the archangel of the sun, Michael, revealed himself to [Jacob] after the battle."[190]

When Jacob receives the name Israel, the nation of Israel is spiritually born, and later, when Benjamin, Jacob's twelfth son, is born, Israel also becomes a nation on earth. God's promise that Abraham's descendants will be like the stars in the sky is fulfilled; the twelve tribes are a reflection of the twelve constellations of the zodiac.

One of Jacob's sons is not like the others. Joseph is the last of the sons born in the old world of Jacob's forefathers and the first born son of Rachel. His father loves him "more than any other of his sons ... and he made him a long sleeved robe" (Gen.37:4), a robe of many colors. Joseph has a soul consciousness of a previous epoch, from a time when the physical world was not looked on with clear senses. Within him lives the old clairvoyant faculties; he has visions and dreams, seeing the spiritual images that surround his soul. The garment that his father gives him is a symbol of his consciousness,[191] and in it can be seen a reflection of the clothes that Gilgamesh receives from Utnapishtim.

Joseph's first dream shows his brothers' sheaves bowing before his (Gen.37:7), and in the second dream the sun, moon, and eleven stars bow down to him (Gen.37:9), showing him elevated above his brothers. Joseph's brothers grow to hate him: their father loves him best of all; he is different from them in his capacity to have dreams, and his dreams show him to be above them. They decide to expel him from their midst and cast him into a pit. "They stripped him of the long- sleeved robe which he was wearing, took him and threw him into a pit. The pit was empty and had not water in it" (Gen.37:23-24). Judah suggests selling him to the Ishmaelites, but some merchants pass by, draw him from the pit and sell him to the Ishmaelites for twenty pieces of silver. The Ishmaelites bring him to Egypt. In this way, Joseph encounters the ancient destiny of Ishmael and as well casts an early reflection of Judas, who, among a group of twelve, betrays Christ for thirty pieces of silver. The past and the future meet in Joseph. Joseph's brothers take his robe, dip it in goat's blood, tear it, and bring it to his father, who believes Joseph has been torn to pieces and devoured by a wild beast.

In Egypt, Joseph is bought by Poliphar, who "put him in charge of his household and entrusted him with all that he had" (Gen.39:4). His master's wife tempts him and seeks her revenge when he rejects her by having him thrown into prison. Again, there is a reflection of the Gilgamesh epic – Ishtar woos Gilgamesh and seeks revenge after he rejects her.

While Joseph is in prison, the Pharaoh's butler and baker are imprisoned and placed in his charge. They each have a dream: the butler dreams of a vine with grapes that are crushed into a cup; the baker dreams of baskets of bread that are eaten by the birds. Joseph interprets these dreams, and all comes to pass as he predicts (Gen.40). Years later the Pharaoh has two dreams which all of the magicians and sages of Egypt cannot interpret. The butler remembers Joseph, who is then brought to interpret the dreams. No longer is Joseph only a dreamer, but he is also a dream interpreter. Through his struggle his consciousness has undergone a change; he carries the ancient clairvoyance as well as the Abraham-power of brain thinking. He is a bearer of intelligence.[192] Through this newly acquired faculty he is released from prison; his destiny changes.

The Pharaoh dreams of seven gaunt and lean cows devouring seven sleek and fat cows (Gen.41:4) and of seven ears of thin and shrivelled corn swallowing seven ears of full and ripe corn (Gen.41:7). Joseph tells him that there is going to be seven years of plenty followed by seven years of famine (Gen 41:29-30), and he explains how to prepare for it so that the country will not be devastated by the famine (Gen.41:34-36). Joseph, from the Abraham-stream, has acquired the skill of calculation and mathematics. He is able to bring economic order to the affairs of the Pharaoh, who is unable to do this since he lacks the capacity of calculation.

The dreams of the birds eating the bread and the dreams of the famine do not only represent external famine, but also a spiritual famine, an approaching end of the spirit revelations flowing in the Egyptian mysteries. The civilization borne by the gods will slowly die out. Through the intellect Joseph is able to prevent Egypt from falling into nothingness; human organization is put in place of divine guidance. Joseph's gift of clairvoyance is used to correct the declining Egyptian culture,[193] and the Pharaoh gives him "authority over the whole land of Egypt" (Gen.41:42).

When the seven years of famine come, "the whole world came to Egypt to buy corn from Joseph" (Gen 41:57), including the sons of Israel, Joseph's brothers, who came and bowed before him. Joseph recognizes his brothers, but they do not recognize him. He sends them back home with sacks of grain, returning their silver to them and asking that they return with Benjamin to prove that they are not spies. The brothers return to Egypt with Benjamin. Again, Joseph fills their sacks with corn and returns their silver. In Benjamin's sack he puts his silver cup. The next morning he sends his steward to bring the "thieves" back. He then reveals himself to his brothers, who go to get their father, and they all return to Egypt to live with Joseph (Gen.42-45).

In Joseph's dreams, in the dreams of the prisoners, in those of the Pharaoh, in the placing of the cup in the sack of corn as well, the image of bread and wine exist; the gift of bread and wine is given to the twelve tribes of Israel, and the way of the future is prepared. The twelve-foldness of the tribes of Israel will be replaced with the ego-bearing twelve-foldness of the disciples, and the cup of suffering of the Israelites will be replaced with the Christian cup of freedom. The gifts of bread and wine will be given to each human ego.[194]

"After Joseph had revealed himself to his brothers, and after all those of his people who had thrust him out had followed him into the sphere of Egyptian rule, a time of learning commenced for Israel, which spanned centuries and was only completed and terminated by Moses."[195]

THE GREEK MYTHS

As the stories of Abraham, Isaac, and Joseph reveal the transition from the sentient soul age to the intellectual soul age, so do the Greek myths.

The story of Prometheus[196] shows how the fire of knowledge and thinking is brought to humanity. Prometheus looks with compassion on men and women, watching them labor and work hard. He thinks that if they have the element that only the Gods know of, the element of fire, that their lives will not be so hard. With fire they can make implements for labor and keep themselves warm. The Gods do not want mankind to have fire, which the Gods created by thought. Prometheus goes against their wishes, takes fire from the altar of Zeus, and brings it to earth. As punishment for going against the will of the Gods, Prometheus is bound to a rock where a vulture tears at his liver each day. Steiner describes Prometheus as the self-conscious man shackled to the earth rock, to the physical body. When the ego entered into and began to work on the astral body, it in turn began to work on the physical body. The gall bladder and the liver developed, the gall being the physical expression of the astral body. In the image of the vulture eating upon Prometheus' liver every day, there is the picture of something arising in the course of evolution that gnaws away at the immortality of mankind. The physical body is chained to the rocks of the earth, and the astral body gnaws away at it.[197]

In the story of the Golden Fleece[198] Jason, the son of Aeson and nephew to King Pelias, is raised in the mountains by the centaur Chiron. Jason learns of the creatures of the forest and their haunts, the knowledge of the stars, and the wisdom that has to do with the ways of the Gods. He grows swift of foot and strong with the spear and bow. When he grows to his full height, Chiron tells him that it is time for him to return to the world of men, and he tells him of his father and how Pelias took the kingship from him. When Jason leaves, Chiron says to him, "Speak harshly to no soul whom you may meet, and stand by the word which you shall speak." Jason comes to the river Anauros, foaming with summer flood. There on the bank sits an old woman waiting to be carried across. The old woman jumps nimbly onto Jason's back, and he steps into the river, stepping up to his knees with the first step and with the second step, up to his waist. The old woman complains that her mantle is getting wet. Jason remembers Chiron's words and pleads for her to be patient. Once the opposite shore is gained, Jason sets down the old woman who proves to be none other than Hera. She blesses him, saying she will help him whenever he is in need. Jason discovers that he lost one of his sandals while crossing the river.

King Pelias had been told by an oracle that he had but one thing to dread - the coming of a half-shod man. When Jason comes into the city, Pelias, seeing a youth wearing only one sandal, remembers the oracle and orders Jason to be brought before him. Jason reveals who he is, and Pelias dares not kill him, so he traps Jason into declaring that he will win the golden fleece and gain fame for himself and the city. When he realizes that he has been tricked, Jason remembers his second promise to Chiron, and he refuses to go back on his word. He has Pelias send a herald around to the princes, calling them to fit out a ship together to undertake the adventure of the golden fleece. Hera stirs the hearts of the princes, and they come. Argus teaches them how to build a ship - the first long ship to sail the seas, fitted with fifty oars, an oar for each hero. They name the ship "Argus."

The fleece that Jason and the heroes are after is the fleece of the ram that carried the children Phrixus and Helle away from the altar where they were about to be sacrificed. Helle fell off the ram into the sea, while Phrixus was carried to the city of Aea. There the ram died, and the king hung the golden fleece upon an oak tree dedicated to Ares, the god of war. It is the king's greatest treasure, guarded by magic powers, and a terrible task awaits anyone who tries to take it away.

Jason and the Argonauts have challenges to face on their way to Aea. They chase away the Harpies that trouble King Phineus, and in exchange for delivering him from the curse of the Gods, he tells them how to maneuver their ship past the Clashing Rocks by following a pigeon who shows them the way. Finally, they come to the end of their journey, to the place where the Golden Fleece is kept. Jason approaches King Aetes and offers him recompense for the fleece, and King Aetes makes him a trial of his bravery; if his bravery wins, he may have the fleece.

Jason must conquer two fire-breathing bulls with feet of brass, yoke them to a plow, plow the field of Ares, and sow the furrows with the teeth of a dragon from which men will spring up. These men he must slay with his spear.

Medea, King Aetes' daughter, decides to help Jason. At night time, she collects the juice from the Promethian flower, the flower that grew from the blood the vulture dropped to earth when it first ate of Prometheus' liver. With the juice of the flower and the juice of other secret herbs, she makes a charm. Jason anoints his body with this charm to protect himself from the breath of the bulls and so that he may have boundless and untiring strength. He also sprinkles some on his shield and sword.

Thus assisted, Jason meets the test that King Aetes set him. King Aetes will not allow Jason to leave peacefully with the fleece, and again Medea helps Jason. Coiled around the oak where the golden fleece hangs there is a deadly serpent with keen and sleepless eyes. Medea sings to it, and it drops from the tree onto the ground. Medea touches its eyes with a juniper branch dipped in a mystic brew, and the serpent's eyes close. Jason takes the fleece, and with Medea beside him, they swiftly leave and set to sea once more.

King Aetes pursues Jason and his crew. Jason and Medea plot to deceive Apsyrtus, her brother who has come to bring her home. Jason slays him, and his blood splashes onto Medea's veil. This killing stirs the wrath of Zeus, and he curses the ship, causing it to wander over the sea until Medea cleanses herself of her brother's blood. They come to the island of Circe. Jason and Medea go to the palace of Circe. She gives them pure water to drink and washes Medea's body and her garments with the spray of the sea, telling her that one day she will meet a wise woman who will tell her what she has to do in her life and what she has to leave undone. This woman Medea must regard.

Tired and full of despair, the Argonauts set off for home once more, but their trials are not yet over. They must pass the Islands of the Sirens; Orpheus sings to them of their own toils so they do not hear the lulling song of the Sirens. They pass the island of the Cattle of the Sun and are caught between Charybdis, the whirlpool, and the rock of Scylla by whom no ship passes safely. There they are caught until Thetis rises from the depths of the sea and guides them safely by. They come to the land of the Phaeacians where they again meet the army of King Aetes. The king of the island will not let them war against each other, and King Aetes' men withdraw. The queen, Queen Arete, tells Medea that she is to forget all the witcheries and enchantments that she knows. Jason and the heroes take to the sea again, only to be cast upon a desert island where the nymphs of the desert tell Jason to watch for Poseidon's great horse. The heroes carry the Argo, following the tracks left in the sand by Poseidon's horse until they come to water once more. They cannot find an outlet from this lake, and their homegoing seems lost to them once more, until Triton comes and leads the Argus to the sea again.

    They come to the island of Crete and, being tired, wish to rest there, but Talos throws rocks at them, not letting them land, until Medea enchants him with her Magic Song, and he falls, breaking the vein that causes his death. The following night a great darkness surrounds the ship, and they know not where they are. When dawn finally comes, they sight the land of Thessaly and would have landed there, but the voice of the ship warns them not to. They sail on, and a great sorrow comes upon Jason for he was not able to land in the home of his father. Finally they come to shore in Corinth.

    The search for the golden fleece, for the ram, is the search for intelligence, for the gift of the age to come, Aries. Jason and the heroes are part god and part human. They are trying to re-establish their connection with the spiritual worlds – to follow the path of initiation. They are initiates striving for self-development through trials and conquests. Their trials are far more difficult after they have attained that which they set out to gain - the golden fleece. Now they must develop themselves further so that the consciousness of their souls can carry this new impulse. After they return home, there is hardly a hero that lives in peace and contentment.

    Heroes again come together for the Trojan war, only now they are fighting against each other. Even the Gods are warring against each other. The war lasts for ten years and is won through the cleverness and the intelligence of Odysseus.[199] The great hero, Achilles, cannot win the war through courage and valor.

Being half-mortal, Achilles is doomed to die, so Thetis, his mother, dips him in the river Styx, rendering his entire body invulnerable, except for the heel that she held him by. After he kills Hector in single combat, Achilles is killed by an arrow from Paris's bow, shot through the vulnerable heel.[200] The valor of Achilles has to step aside to allow the intelligence of Odysseus to bring the conquest to an end. Achilles lacks the power to cross the threshold of the dawning age. Odysseus and Achilles are reflections of Jacob and Esau. Esau, whose heel had been grasped at birth had to step aside for Jacob to carry humanity forward.[201]

After the end of the Trojan war, Odysseus[202] travels for another ten years before he reaches his homeland, and faces many of the trials that Jason and the Argonauts encountered: the island of Circe, the Sirens, the two faces of evil (Scylla and Charybdis), and the island of the Cattle of the Sun. However, as Jason and his crew avoided many of these dangers, Odysseus goes forward to face them and overcomes them through his intelligence.

When caught by the Cyclops Polyphemus, Odysseus gets him drunk, blinds him, and then ties his men to the underbellies of the sheep, so that they can pass by him undetected. With the help of Hermes, Odysseus is able to outwit Circe, who like Ishtar, changes men into the shapes of animals, and she has to free his men from her spell. Rather than avoiding the Sirens, Odysseus blocks his men's hearing with wax and ties himself to the mast of the ship so that he can hear the songs of the Sirens without being caught by them. He passes unassisted by Scylla and Charybdis, losing six of his men to the monster. He alone of his men is able to resist killing the Cattle of the Sun, for which all of his men die, and he arrives alone at the Palace of King Alcinous and Queen Arete, where Jason had also found a haven. They help him return to Ithaca. When Odysseus arrives home, the world he returns to is not the same as the one he had left twenty years earlier. His home is overrun with men who are courting his wife. He and his son set up a challenge for these princes. They must string the bow of Odysseus and shoot an arrow through the space between twelve axes set up in two rows. This feat is similar to the once set before Rama that won him his bride. Through this challenge Odysseus wins his wife away from her suitors. Penelope does not believe that Odysseus has returned, and she sets him a test to prove himself, which he does by knowing the secret of the fashioning of his bed.

When Odysseus built his bedchamber, he fastened the headpost to an olive tree, lopping the branches, trimming the trunk, and fastening the bedframe to the post. Around the tree, the bedchamber was built. This "tree" construction also exists in other myths. In the Norse myths, King Volsung has his hall built around Branstokk with its branches above the rafters,[203] and as seen earlier, the king of Byblos has the tree that encloses the coffin of Osiris serve as a pillar in his palace. The pictures that lie behind the words of the myths are not unfamiliar to the people of different cultures.

The story of the Odyssey is the story of a path of initiation. The Greek myths give a picture of the transition into and development of the age of the intellectual soul. There is a greater awareness of the world of the senses with a fading awareness of the spiritual world. The physical world is enjoyed by the Greeks so much so that when Odysseus meets Achilles in the Land of Hades, Achilles says to him: "I would rather be on earth, alive, the slave of some poor wretched man, and live in drudgery and want, than rule here, king of all the dead."[204] The heroes gain a greater awareness of their individuality. Their part-divine, part-human nature reveals the divine and human aspects of humanity. Their adventures are quests where they seek to develop their higher self by overcoming hindrances in earthly life. The overcoming of the Cyclops by Odysseus represents the passing of the old faculty of clairvoyance, a faculty that had to be blinded for the new consciousness to arise. When Theseus kills the minotaur,[205] it is the end of the age of Taurus and the beginning of the age of Aries. By following a thread (logical thought), Theseus succeeds at his trial, and intelligence becomes the important faculty.

After the Trojan war, Odysseus returns to a changed old world, while Aeneas[206] sets off to start a new world in Italy. Juno, or Hera in Greek mythology, is unhappy with the Trojans, because Paris gave the apple to Aphrodite, choosing her as the most beautiful woman.[207] Juno creates a storm that casts Aeneas's ship onto the shores of Carthage. Here Aeneas stays until Mercury comes to him and reminds him that this is not his destiny - there is another kingdom which is to be his. In the night Aeneas leaves Carthage. Dido, who has grown to love him, full of despair, takes her life.

AENEAS

Aeneas, like Odysseus, travels to the underworld, and he, too, meets the heroes who died in the Trojan war. He also meets his father, whom three times he tries to clasp but cannot. While travelling through the Land of Hades, Aeneas sees the "souls who are destined to live in the body a second time and at Lethe's wave they are drinking the waters which abolish care and give enduring release from memory." Anchises explains to Aeneas why souls desire the light of day. He tells of how the cosmos is strengthened by Spirit and Mind working in them, how men, beasts, birds, and creatures of the ocean are created from Spirit and Mind. Their origin is of Heaven, and the body is the cause of fear, desire, sorrow, and joy. At death not all evils and ills of the body pass from the soul, so souls pay in punishment for their old offences, until all the hardened corruption is removed, and there remains but a spark of elemental fire. When the circle of a thousand years has passed, God calls forth the souls. They drink from the river Lethe, erasing all memory so that a wish to reenter bodily life may dawn. Anchises then shows Aeneas the line of descendants to follow him down to Romulus, who will cause Rome to be illustrious and "extend her authority to the breadth of the earth and her spirit to the height of Olympus. She shall build her single wall round seven citadels." Showing him what lies in the future, Anchises asks Aeneas: "Can we now hesitate to assert our valour by our deeds? Can any fear now prevent us from taking our stand on Italy's soil?" Aeneas has revealed to him the kings of Rome and what they will bring to the country of Rome, and the arts and skills that will be developed by the Romans. Anchises shows his son each sight to kindle his imagination with a passion for the glory to be.

Aeneas lands in Latium. King Latinus has a daughter to whom he may not marry any man of his race, but only to a foreigner. The future of Latium depends on a new strain mixing with the old and exalting them to the stars. This has been revealed to Latinus through his father's oracle. Lavinia is offered to Aeneas, and a great war breaks out for Turnus wishes to marry her. Turnus dies in battle, and Aeneas marries Lavinia.

Through his visit to the underworld, Aeneas learns the secrets of creation, the true nature of mankind, and the mysteries of reincarnation. He is shown the future, so that he may have the courage to fulfill his destiny. The fulfillment of his destiny leads to the Greco/Roman civilization, the fourth Post-Atlantean epoch, the time of the intellectual soul.

MOSES

As Anchises shows Aeneas what lies ahead in the future, so does Jacob show his sons what will happen to them in the days to come. In the course of time, all the generations who followed Joseph into Egypt die, and the Israelites become fruitful and prolific. A new king ascends the throne in Egypt, and he decides to ensure that the Israelites do not increase any further. He makes them slaves and orders that all the Hebrew male children be killed at birth. When Moses is born, his mother hides him in a rush basket among the reeds on the Nile. The Pharaoh's daughter finds him and adopts him. In this way Moses becomes initiated into the Egyptian mysteries. When he grows up, Moses sees an Egyptian strike one of his fellow Hebrews. Moses strikes the Egyptian back, killing him. The Pharaoh hears of the incident and tries to put Moses to death, but he manages to escape. God appears to Moses and tells him to lead the Israelites out of Egypt. Moses returns to Egypt and asks the Pharaoh to let his people go. The Pharaoh refuses, and God sends ten plagues against the Egyptians. One last plague is brought upon the Pharaoh: the Lord goes through Egypt, striking the first born of all throughout the land. Where the Israelites have marked their two door posts with the blood of sheep, God passes over their houses.

The Egyptians urge the Israelites out of the country. The Pharaoh is made obstinate by the Lord, and he pursues the Israelites. Seeing the Egyptians in pursuit of them, the Hebrews ask Moses to let them be slaves rather than force them to die in the wilderness. When they come to the sea, Moses stretches his hand over the sea, and the waters are torn apart. The Israelites go through on dry ground between two walls of water. The Egyptians follow behind, but before they cross, Moses stretches forth his hand once more, and the waters return to their usual place. Not one Egyptian is left alive (Exodus.1-14).

The Exodus of the Israelites from Egypt marks the end of the sentient soul age. Moses represents the first historical figure. As cosmic time came to an end, mythological time ends, and historical time begins.

The transition from the third Post-Atlantean epoch to the fourth is a time of great change. The Greeks return home after a long war to find a new world; the Trojans set off to establish a new world in Latium; and the Hebrews set off for the Promised Land. The trials that these people undergo on their journeys bring about a change in consciousness that allows the new age to begin.

GRECO/ROMAN EPOCH

The fourth Post-Atlantean epoch, the Greco/Roman epoch, is a time when mankind came even further into contact with the physical plane; mankind completed its descent from the spiritual world and fully incarnated on the earth. In this intellectual soul period, for the first time humanity became capable of thinking for itself, which led to the creation of philosophy and abstract thinking, the questioning of long held assumptions, and traditional religious teachings. The gods of the Greeks were memories of the gods who were companions to mankind in Atlantis. What the Atlanteans felt and experienced clairvoyantly reappeared in the fourth Post-Atlantean epoch as the pantheon.[208] Not only did mankind see the script of the gods in the physical world, but man's own spiritual individuality was inserted into the objective world. In Greece this manifested in sculptures where the artists worked not from models, but from the experience of their own etheric forces, resulting in statuary of unique beauty that always portrayed the gods and goddesses in the prime of life, for the etheric body does not grow old.[209] The Greeks felt an impulse to create within the world of the senses an expression of the spiritual world in a perfect form. The Greek temples became the dwelling place in the physical world for the Greek gods; the temples became the physical bodies where the etheric bodies of the gods and goddesses felt at home.[210]

The people of the Greco/Roman epoch "cultivated the physical life of the senses so that it blossomed forth under their hands. In so doing they ... condemned themselves to a shadow-like existence after death."[211] For the Greek people life after death was the existence of the Shades, and Achilles' statement of preferring to be a beggar on earth than a king in the realm of the Shades was an expression of a real feeling of truth.

As well as the Greek civilization, the Roman civilization came to birth and dominance in the fourth Post-Atlantean epoch. The Roman people resulted from two races of people - the original people of Latium and Aeneas and his followers who journeyed to Latium after the Trojan war.

From the descendants of Aeneas and Lavinia come twin brothers, Romulus and Remus. Mars, the god of war, is the father of the twins, and Ilia their mother. A few days after their birth, Romulus and Remus are exposed on the banks of the Tiber River. A she-wolf comes out of the forest and miraculously suckles them. They are sheltered by a kindly shepherd, Faustulus, who takes them home, and he and his wife, Acca Lerentia, raise them. After restoring their grandfather to the throne, Romulus and Remus set off to found a city near the hills where they grew up. In order to consult the gods, Romulus chooses the Palatine, the home of his childhood; Remus occupies the Aventine. From the hilltops they watch for a sign from the gods indicating which one of them will name the city they are to found. Remus first sees six vultures cross the sky, but the gods favor "Romulus by sending him the extraordinary omen of a flight of twelve vultures," awarding him the glory of founding the city. Romulus immediately plows a furrow around the Palatine; the cast up earth symbolizes a wall, the furrow a moat, and where there are to be gates, the plow is raised to allow a passage. Remus jeers mockingly at the "wall" of earth and the contemptible trench and jumps across them. Romulus falls upon him and slays him as a victim saying: "So perish all who ever cross my walls!" Romulus gathers into the city the young neighboring shepherds, the outlaws, and homeless and stateless people of Latium. However, having to ensure a future for the city, where there are no women among its founding citizens, Romulus arranges impressive games inviting the families of the neighboring cities. During the games a signal is given whereby the Romans fall upon the visitors' daughters, carrying them into their homes. Thus arises the first Roman war. The Sabine women, who are well treated by their husbands, throw themselves between the contending forces and restore peace.

After Romulus founds the city, ensures the survival of its population, plans the administration by establishing a senate consisting of the heads of families, and an assembly of people, he vanishes in the midst of a thunderstorm before the eyes of the whole populace. The voice of the people proclaim that he has become a god.[212]

The founding of Rome has a number of elements of a warrior nation: Mars, the god of war, sires the twins; the establishment of the first ruler is based on the flight of vultures; the crime of a brother's murder stains the first king. This crime is seen as a kind of original sin, whose consequence must bring the ruin to the city by driving her sons to mutual slaughter. A curse hangs over Rome and she is no more at peace with the gods than she is at peace with men at her birth. The Greeks, too, experienced "crimes" at the beginning of the intellectual soul age: Theseus brought about the death of his father by neglecting to change the black sail of his ship to a white sail; Orestes killed his mother to avenge his father's death; and Oedipus brought strife to Thebes by marrying his mother. However, where the Greeks felt that the normal workings of religious institutions would remove the greatest of sins, the Romans suffered religious anxiety over the death of Remus and trembled, awaiting a divine portent.[213]

The figure of Romulus is an amalgamation of different elements: lawgiver, warrior, and priest. He is "a direct interpreter of the will of the gods, a kind of human fetish possessed of magic powers, an invincible warrior by the very nature of this grace with which he is endowed, and the supreme dispenser of justice to his people."[214] These different elements are united in Romulus through the "divine sanction" of his rule, a grace that remains throughout the subsequent course of Roman history. As mankind descended further into the physical realm during the intellectual soul age, they forgot their spiritual origins, and instead of worshipping the gods whom they were no longer directly aware of, they worshipped men, deifying them either in their lifetimes or after their deaths. The Romans deified and worshipped their emperors.[215]

The history of Rome is a story of the increased materialization of the world through the intellect, as shown in the building of roads, the aqueducts, and the great army. The Roman achievements stem from their deeper penetration of the ego into the physical body. One of the consequences of this penetration is the stress laid by the Romans on character and individuality. While the Greek heroes were remembered for their talents, the Roman heroes were remembered for their character. Horatius, who with a few companions held the enemy at bay at a bridge while being hopelessly outnumbered, cast himself into the river, surfaced again, and was hailed a hero for his selflessness for his nation.

Roman law was the first law to grant legal rights to individuals, even the right for individuals to dispose of their property as they saw fit after their death with the institution of the "will."[216]

The Greco-Roman epoch brought three major new developments to civilization: the development of individuality and a greater awareness of self; the conquest of the physical world and the loss of the awareness of the origin of mortal beings; and the birth of thinking.

In preparation for the full incarnation of the "I" it was necessary for mankind to be told how this "I" was to act when it became incorporated into the physical body. This was the purpose of the Ten Commandments that were given to Moses at Mt. Sinai (Exodus.19-20); he was given a series of moral principles which mankind was not yet capable of evolving from within their own being at the beginning of the intellectual soul age. During this era, these principles became internalized, so that humanity experienced "sin" when they went against any of the injunctions.[217]

Moses leads the Hebrew people out of Egypt, but he dies before they reach the promised land. Joshua leads them into their new land (Joshua.1:1-3). In the Old Testament, the stories of Ruth, Saul, David, Solomon, and the stories of the Judges and Kings, are the stories of the intellectual soul age. The story of David and Goliath parallels the story of Odysseus and the Cyclops. Goliath, a giant symbolizing a time when the etheric forces extended beyond the physical body of mankind, is slain by a stone sinking into his forehead. Similarly, Odysseus overcame the Cyclops when he blinded the single eye in the middle of the Polyphemus' forehead.

Solomon is granted a heart so wise and so understanding that there were none like him before. When two women come to him to decide who is the rightful mother of a child, he is able to recognize the true mother through his wisdom. The "responsive soul," another name that Steiner gives to the intellectual soul, is also translated as "mind warmed by a loving heart,"[218] and is apparent in King Solomon.

In the works of the Hebrew people there is a "gradual recognition of the truth that the time was coming when men would assume full responsibility for their acts, ... that mere obedience to the Law was to be transformed into full inner recognition of moral responsibility."[219] The evolution of mankind through the Post-Atlantean epochs is a descent out of the spiritual worlds into the physical world, until at the Greco/Roman epoch there comes the point of the greatest descent into the physical realm. Now the task of humanity is to acquire consciousness of the spiritual worlds through individual effort. Through the Christ-impulse that enters the earth in the middle of the Earth incarnation, fully incarnated humanity is able to ascend again into the spiritual world, carrying with them that which has been gained in the world of the senses. At a time when the Romans were building their empire through great wars and conquest and were involved in worshipping their emperors as gods, the Christ-impulse entered earthly evolution.

> With the resurrection the possibility was given to man to fulfill the mission originally purposed for him by the gods and to become a truly free being. As long as men had an actual perception of the spiritual worlds and knew from their own experience and knowledge that they were guided by higher beings, then they could not be truly free. It was necessary that this knowledge should be taken away from them and the spiritual worlds darkened if they were to find within themselves their own higher being, which, from the time of the Mystery of Golgotha, had become capable of being filled by the Christ.... The Mystery of Golgotha took place at the very center of earth evolution ... and the upward evolution of man following the Mystery should continue slowly until the end of earth evolution.[220]

THE ARTHURIAN LEGENDS

The beginning of the upward evolution of mankind is apparent in the stories of King Arthur and the Knights of the Round Table. After the fall of the Holy Roman Empire, Roman law no longer applies and savagery arises in the world. King Arthur goes forth into the world to tame the wildness and to bring peace to the realm. As Moses brought the Ten Commandments to the Hebrews, in the middle of the Dark Ages, Arthur brings a model of chivalry and "right striving," developing the heroic character with qualities of strength, valor, justice, modesty, loyalty to superiors and family, courtesy to equals, compassion to weakness, and devotion to the church. As well, as Sir Tristram explains, "bravery should be tempered by wisdom,"[221] and Iseult expresses, "the very purpose of a knight is to fight on behalf of a lady."[222]

The birth of Arthur is cloaked in the magic and mystery of Merlin. Merlin causes King Uther to look like Gorlois, Duke of Tintagil, so that he can gain access to Igraine's bed. Igraine then gives birth to Arthur. When he is born, Arthur is carried away by Merlin and is raised in secrecy. He is taught the mysteries of nature by Merlin and the ways of war by Sir Ector, his stepfather.

Arthur is brought to the throne of Britain under the auspices of the church, through the Archbishop, as well as under the auspices of the elemental forces, through Merlin. After King Uther dies, the ambitious barons fight for the throne until the whole of Britain stands in jeopardy. The Archbishop of Canterbury summons the nobility to London on Christmas morning, promising that the true succession to the British throne will be revealed miraculously at that time. Merlin causes a large stone to appear before the church. On this stone there is an anvil, and thrust into the anvil is a sword. The anvil is inscribed with letters of gold: "Who so pulls this sword out of this stone and anvil is the rightful king born of all Britain." Unseen by anyone, Arthur draws the sword from the stone, which he then replaces to draw it out again in front of witnesses. The nobles protest "against one so young, and of ignoble blood, succeeding the throne,"[223] so the trial is repeated on the Christian festivals of Candlemas, Easter, and Pentecost, when Arthur is finally accepted and acknowledged as the king of Britain.

The sword that appears in the stone is a mirror picture of the sword that Odin drove deep into the trunk of Branstokk saying: "To him who can draw forth this sword I give it as a gift, and he shall find that never has he borne a better weapon."[224] It was Sigmund that the Allfather had chosen to be his own warrior.

Arthur continues to be guided and counselled by Merlin and the Archbishop. With the help of Merlin, Arthur acquires the magic sword, Excalibur, from the Lady of the Lake, along with the scabbard that prevents the loss of blood regardless of how seriously the one who wears it is wounded. Excalibur replaces the sword from the stone, which was broken in a battle. Excalibur leads Arthur to glory.

When Arthur marries Gwynevere, he gains the Round Table. The Table had been made by Merlin for King Uther, and it was fashioned in a circle, so that when the knights were seated at it, "no one of them should be lower at the board than another, and there should be no envy or jealousy between them."[225] Merlin devised the Table as a "symbol of the wholeness of virtue."[226] Arthur conceives of "the idea of founding an order of knights sworn to be loyal to him, who should sit at the famous table ... to be known as the Knights of the Round Table."[227]

Through the Knights of the Round Table, Arthur tries "to create on earth a community able to reflect the harmony of the stars. The King and Queen with their twelve knights represent the sun and moon in their relationship with the twelve signs of the Zodiac. On earth there is everywhere chaos, but in the heavens a divine order is made manifest which they strive to reflect."[228] The Round Table represents world brotherhood.

After the wedding feast of King Arthur and Gwynevere an unusual event happens; a white hart gallops into the hall, followed by a white brachet and thirty pairs of black hounds, and a young noblewoman rides into the hall crying for help, only to be seized and carried away by a knight on a powerful charger. Thus begins the first quests of the Knights of the Round Table.

The quests of the Knights are quests of self-development, to prove their right to be a Knight through deeds of courage, valor, and honour. The Knights go off seeking adventure in the world, which they find at every turn; wherever they go there is evil to overcome. Often they journey together, supporting each other in the conquests that they face, going out into the world and returning to the Round Table at each feast of Pentecost.

One Whitsun a hermit appears at King Arthur's court asking about the empty seat at the table, Siege Perelous. He prophesies that he who is to fill that seat will be born that year, and he shall win the Holy Grail. After the feast Sir Launcelot goes off seeking adventure, and he comes to a prison tower where a lady is perpetually scalded by boiling water "until the greatest knight on earth should come to her rescue."[229] After rescuing her, he then meets King Pelles, a descendant of Joseph of Arimathea. While eating with him Launcelot has his first vision of the Holy Grail. Through enchantment, King Pelles has Launcelot get his daughter, Elaine, with child for "it had been prophesied that the son she would bear him, Sir Galahad, would be the purest knight of all time and win the Holy Grail." The order of things begins to change.

Some years later, at the feast of Pentecost, when all the Knights are assembled, in the river that passes by the castle, a red marble stone appears, floating in the water. Into the marble a finely made sword with a jewelled hilt is thrust. There is an inscription on the hilt: "Never shall man take me hense but only he by whose side I ought to hang and he shall be the best knight of the world." Arthur suggests that Launcelot is the best knight in the world and surely this is his sword. Launcelot knows in his heart that the sword is not for him: "Sire, I know that this is not my sword and that I am not the best knight in the world. Further, if any but the rightful owner should touch the sword, he will receive from it a wound from which he may never recover. And with the coming of the best knight in the world will start the quest of the Holy Grail." With the quest for the Holy Grail, the Round Table will be dispersed as the Knights go in search of it. Once again, a change to the order of things is brought about by a sword in a stone.

Galahad arrives at court, claims the Siege Perelous and the sword from the marble stone. Launcelot is told that there is now a knight greater than he is, but of sinful knights, he is still the greatest. That evening the Holy Grail passes through Camelot, "covered with white samite." Sir Gawain, wanting to see the Grail uncovered, vows to search for it for a year and a day. The fellowship of the Round Table is irremediably broken; never again will the complete fellowship gather around the Round Table. Each Knight goes off in the direction of his choice. Where before the companions travelled together, now they must meet their challenges on their own. Where adventures used to meet them at every turn, now they do not meet with any. The nature of the quest for the Holy Grail is different than the nature of the quests from before the Grail. The nature of the quest "is the challenge of evil which each knight must transcend in order to participate in the holy mysteries." The adventures the Knights were accustomed to often involved the killing of men, and the quest of the Holy Grail means conquests other than this. No longer does self-development come from gaining conquests in the outer world, but now it comes from gaining conquests in the inner world of one's own nature. Worldly renown cannot help the Knights now for it cannot avail in matters of the spirit.

Of those who quest for the Grail, it is Launcelot who has the greatest struggle; in body he is the greatest knight, but because of his defilement, many surpass him spiritually. Soon after his first vision of the Holy Grail, Launcelot goes mad, wandering in the forest until he once again arrives at the court of King Pelles, and through the Holy Grail his reason is restored to him. He comes to refer to himself as "the knight who has trespassed."

Through his dreams and with the help of hermits and holy men, Launcelot comes to see his true nature: "Sir Launcelot, you are harder than stone, more bitter than wood, and more barren than a fig tree. Go hence for you are not worthy of this holy place." Like Geirrod, Launcelot has used the gifts that God has given him for the furtherance of his own sin, but unlike Geirrod, who had to die because of his sin, since the Mystery of Golgotha, Launcelot does not have to die for his sin. However, because of his sin, he is described as being harder than stone. He has courage, beauty, intelligence, the capacity to distinguish good from evil, and the knowledge of what conduct is pleasing to God, yet he shuts out God through his sin, and in sin there is no sweetness; therefore, he is more bitter than wood. Launcelot is like the fig tree that Jesus cursed, which grew copious leaves, but was barren of fruit. In the presence of the Holy Grail, Launcelot is denied its mysteries. He dares to try to discover the mysteries of the Grail while in a state of mortal sin, and he cannot succeed.

Launcelot confesses his sin of loving "the Queen for many years, caring nothing for God, failing to thank Him for his victories, wishing only to gain the queen's love and praise." For his penance, he wears a hair shirt next to his skin, to enhance his virtue, and he abstains from meat and wine while on the quest. He is now nearer to his goal and more ready to perceive it than before.

Launcelot must continue to bear the burden of his sin; again, he falls into error. When he comes across a battle between an army of black knights and an army of white knights, he joins the side of the black knights, for they seem to be losing. The white knights shame him on the battlefield and drag him from it. A recluse in a chapel helps Launcelot see that his renown in battle cannot help him in spiritual matters. The black knights he was supporting are those bound to earthly sin, while the white knights were those free of sin, acting in a state of grace. Launcelot is warned that he is not of the blessed; he "will fight only in the cause of evil to gain worldly glory, to assuage [his] own pride and vainglory, and those things are not worth a pear."

Launcelot eventually comes to where the Holy Grail is kept, a castle guarded by two lions. He draws his sword against them, until he is reminded by a dwarf that his sword and armour cannot prevail against the will of the Lord. Launcelot sheaths his sword, crosses himself, and enters the castle. He comes to the room where the Grail is, but when he tries to enter it, he is forbidden. He watches the priest performing the consecration of the mass, and above the priest there are three men, two of them setting the third to rest on the hands of the priest as he raises them. Feeling that the man is about to fall, Launcelot rushes into the room, sure that it is no sin to give succour to one in need, only to be burned by a fiery breath. He falls into a swoon and remains prostrate for twenty-four days – one day for each year that he has sinned.

When Sir Gawain rides out on the quest, he tries to ride with Galahad, but a monk tells him that Galahad will not accept his companionship, for he is wicked, and Galahad is blessed. Since he was knighted, Gawain has followed the path of sin. This is apparent when he and his brothers kill the seven knights that Galahad, who is without sin, overcame single handedly without killing. When the hermit tries to direct Gawain in the penance he should do, he replies, "No, good father, for a knight in the course of his adventures surely suffers enough in body and soul."

While travelling with Sir Ector, the two knights come across a chapel, where they sleep for the night. During the night they each have a dream, and in the morning they share a common vision of an arm moving slowly across the chapel. Over the arm lays a bridle, and in the hand, a bright burning candle is clasped. They find a holy man to interpret these visions. Gawain's dream reveals that only three of the knights will fulfill the quest of the Holy Grail, and of all the knights that set out on the quest, only some will return, exhausted. The others will die, some at the hands of their fellow knights. Ector's dream reveals the penance that Launcelot is willing to do for the sake of the quest, yet the grace of God is withdrawn from him, and he is impotent in the presence of the Grail. The holy man also explains the vision in the chapel: "The arm was the charity of the Holy Ghost, the bridle signified abstinence; for he who is in a state of grace is held close so that he does not fall into sin again. The bright-burning candle was the light of our Lord Jesus Christ. When the voice spoke and said that these tokens had failed you, the meaning was that lacking charity, virtue, and faith, you shall not achieve the Holy Grail." Again the holy man tries to counsel Gawain, comparing him to an old tree of which the leaves, fruit, and sap have withered. All he has left to offer God is a dry husk. Gawain does not stay, but rides on. Unwilling to admit his state of sin and need for penance, neither Sir Gawain nor Sir Ector fulfill the quest of the Holy Grail.

Sir Bors has his first vision of the Grail at King Pelles' court when Galahad is but a child. Afterwards Bors confesses of his single sin, and in the night he is confronted with several challenges: an illumined spear wounds him in the shoulder; he is challenged by a knight; arrows fly in through the windows and doors, wounding him where he is exposed; a lion appears that he beheads; and a dragon and leopard appear fighting each other. These are not challenges that Sir Bors has to face in the outer world; they are challenges of his own inner world that he encounters in the privacy of his own room. When the experiences end, an old man appears, telling him of the story of Joseph of Arimathea. He also tells him that there are no further adventures here for him and that he has done well and will do better in the future.

Sir Bors also wears a garment of chastisement, a red coat, and he eats only bread and water while on the quest. He, too, has dreams and experiences that guide him on his quest. As well he is faced with temptations. Lucifer, disguised as a beautiful heiress, tries to tempt Sir Bors and coerce him into sin to circumvent his achievement of the Holy Grail. Sir Bors does not succumb to this temptation.

Percivale is also tempted by Lucifer disguised as a woman who has been disinherited because of her pride. From this experience, Percivale learns how the Lord had disinherited Lucifer, the most beautiful of the angels, for his sin of pride.

As Galahad, Percivale, and Sir Bors travel together to the castle where the Holy Grail is kept, cosmic events in the evolution of humanity are revealed to them, showing once again that the facts of cosmic evolution repeat themselves in humanity's inner knowledge and are revealed through stories.

The ship that the three knights are travelling on contains a bed. The three spindles that support the canopy are of three different colors: blood red, snow white, and emerald green. These are the natural colors of the wood and are not painted on. Sir Percivale's sister reveals to them the mystery of the spindles:

> When Eve gathered apples from the tree, for the eating of which both she and Adam were to be cast out of Eden, she also took one of the boughs, which delighted her for its freshness. Having no box in which to keep it, she planted the bough in the ground, and God willed that it should grow into a tree. And because Eve was a maid at the time, the tree grew white.
>
> Then God came to Adam and commanded him to love Eve and enter her in the flesh and procreate his kind. Adam took Eve as she lay beneath the tree which she had planted, and their son Abel was conceived. While Adam and Eve engaged in the act of love, the tree grew green, and for many years remained that color.
>
> Then, beneath the tree, Cain slew Abel, and the color changed again, this time to red, the color of Abel's blood.

This is a revelation of the transition from Lemuria to Atlantis where Cain, the last born of Lemuria, was born prior to the curse of the fall and where Abel, the first born of the Atlantean age, was born after the curse of the fall. As revealed here, Abel is the first offspring born from the duality of the sexes.

When the young noblewoman and the three knights ride through the forest, they follow four lions into a chapel. Three of the lions change form; in the chapel there is a lion, an eagle, an ox, and a man.

Rudolf Steiner explains that in the evolution of the human form, the physical body, the etheric body, the astral body, or the ego could work especially strongly, dominating over the other three members. Through this, four human types developed. For those people in whom the physical nature worked especially strongly there appeared the shape of the bull; what was governed mainly by the physical body remained at the stage of the bull. Where the etheric body was strongly marked, the heart region was especially powerful, and here the human group was preserved in the shape of the lion. The human stage where the astral was overpowering was preserved in the eagle; the predominant astrality raised itself from the earth as a bird. Where the ego grew strong, a being evolved that united the three other natures in the form of a sphinx with a human face. In Atlantean times, the human shape gradually constructed itself out of the eagle, lion, and bull natures. These transmuted themselves into the full human form.[230] Within the stories of King Arthur, there are mirror images of events that took place during the Atlantean age.

After the quest of the Holy Grail is achieved, the peace that Arthur brought during his reign ends. The knights turn against and fight each other. A snake again is the creature that brings about the end of the world as it is; it is the cause of a battle that brings the death of Mordred and Arthur. Excalibur is returned to the Lady of the Lake, and the golden age of chivalry comes to an end. Many of the knights take up the life of a hermit.

CONSCIOUSNESS SOUL AGE

Throughout the fourth, fifth, and sixth centuries AD there existed a preparation for a new epoch which actually only began in the fifteenth century and which we are still living in today.[231] This is the fifth Post-Atlantean or Aryan epoch, the consciousness soul age. The tasks of humanity in this age are to gain a new attitude towards the material world and to gain conscious knowledge of the spiritual world. Humanity is no longer dependent upon divine guidance, and each person must take his or her own self-development in hand. Reliance on the group to carry humanity forward is no longer adequate, and individualization is stronger. Each person's quest is his own as seen in the Arthurian legends after the appearance of the Holy Grail. Individuals need to confront their own fears and doubts. Evil does not only exist without, but also within. It is a time of greater isolation and separation. The power of the hindering forces are greater at this time, with Lucifer deluding mankind into believing that they are like gods, and Ahriman persuading humanity to think that they are purely human without any divine element and that the world is there for them to use. The force of Ahriman leads to materialism. The task of humanity is to walk the path between these two hindering forces. It is not predestined that Ahriman and Lucifer will be defeated, for their defeat can only come about through free choice. This goal must be reached in freedom. The proper task of the consciousness soul is to come to terms with the material world and to be able to observe it objectively.[232]

In the fifth Post-Atlantean epoch there is a reawakening of that which took place in the third Post-Atlantean epoch, the Egypto/Chaldean epoch; "in superearthly connections, there are mysterious threads between Egyptian culture and that of today."[233] From the image of the Madonna and child, a thread can lead back into Egyptian time to Isis and Horus. The mysteries of Isis, the lovable goddess, reappear in the Madonna. "The Madonna is a remembrance of Isis; Isis appears again in the Madonna."[234]

Another thread that connects Egyptian and present time is the way Egyptians handled their dead; the Egyptians were concerned with preserving the physical form as long as possible. Through embalming and mummification the dead were bound to the physical plane. As a result of this the soul, after death, continued to be bound to the physical body, and the body became important to the soul. The attachment to the body, and the fruit of looking down upon it after death appear now "in the fifth period, in the inclination that souls have today to lay great weight upon the outer physical life.... Through this man learned to love the physical world; through this it is often said today that the only important thing is the physical body between birth and death."[235]

The perception of the spiritual world that was strong in the sentient soul age of the Egypto/Chaldean epoch must be reacquired consciously without losing the ability to perceive the earth and understand it from a material point of view.[236] In the first Post-Atlantean epoch, Old Indian, the unity of earthly evolution was remembered. In the Old Persian epoch the duality of good and evil were conceived; in ancient Egypt the trinity; and in the Greco/Roman epoch the godlike figures of Atlantis were remembered. In the fifth Post-Atlantean epoch, however, nothing can be remembered, thereby allowing godlessness to make great headway. The fifth period must look ahead, rather than to the past,/ to when all the gods must arise again. The consciousness must become apocalyptic.[237]

The historical events that occurred in the 14th and 15th centuries show the passing of an old age and the birth of a new one: religious life was in decay; the Hundred Years War was raging in France; the mission of Joan of Arc separated England and France; the Black Death raged; and the medieval civilization and the feudal and manorial systems collapsed. At the beginning of the consciousness soul age the recapitulation of the sentient soul development was apparent in the Italian Renaissance and in the 17th century. When France became the cultural leader of Europe, the intellectual soul age was recapitulated. The true bearers of the new age of the consciousness soul were the British, with steps being taken towards the enforcement of equal rights for all people, the system of government by representation, religious tolerance, and industrial civilization. The task of the German people at this time was to bring about the full development of the "I." In the twentieth century, the Americans are expected to to carry forward the full development of the consciousness soul.[238]

PARZIVAL

The consciousness soul age "has the task of building the bridge from one person to another consciously by true perception and recognition of the 'I' of others."[239] Parzival can be seen as the forerunner of modern man; he carries the impulse for the consciousness soul age. He is slow to grow wise, but through his steadfast endeavours he takes on his own self-development, until he succeeds in transforming his lower nature and is able to become the Grail King. Parzival[240] ventures off into the world with so little self-knowledge that he does not even know his own name. When he meets Sigune for the first time, she tells him his name. She is able to see his true nature and greets him with: "You have much to commend you.... The day will come, I know, when you will be blessed with good fortune." This is the beginning of Parzival's path of gaining self knowledge.

Growing up in isolation, "reared in the wilds of Soltane," those around Parzival conceal from him the knowledge of chivalry until he can think for himself; he grows up ignorant of the world around him. Through his naivete and innocence, Parzival is unaware of the grief he causes when he goes out into the world. He does not know that his leaving causes his mother's death. He does not know the suffering that his actions bring to Jeschute. The distress that Cunneware innocently suffers because of him angers Parzival to the core. In his innocence Parzival fights the Red Knight for his armour, and in anger he clutches his javelin and kills his opponent. Later, on reaching years of discretion, Parzival wishes he had not done it. After gaining the armour, Parzival does not know how to remove it. He does not know that the Order of Chivalry forbids the use of javelins. He has to be taught how to use a sword and how to maneuver behind his shield, while watching for the chance to strike at his enemy. However, in his brief encounter with the world, Parzival does recognize that he has been offended by a knight who struck a young lady who honoured him with her laughter. He feels greatly disgraced and rides off in shame, covering a distance in one day that "an old campaigner" would only cover in two.

Parzival reaches Gurnemanz, and prompted by youthful ignorance, he quickly says: "My mother asked me to seek advice of a man whose locks are grey." Gurnemanz welcomes him and begins his training, teaching him how to behave in the world and advising him to "not ask many questions." Parzival, believing that "it was noble ambition that led to triumph in this life and the next" takes leave of Gurnemanz to win fame as a knight.

Soon after leaving Gurnemanz, Parzival comes to a swinging bridge that his horse will not cross. Dismounting, he leads his horse over the rickety bridge. This incident is comparable to that of Odysseus passing between Scylla and Charybdis, and "expresses in an imaginative form the quality of balance and the ability to avoid extremes"[241] that Parzival has now gained. The task of humanity in the consciousness soul age is to walk the narrow path between the hindering forces of Lucifer and Ahriman. Parzival has developed the power of judgment, an inner balance, and the ability to make the right decision.

No longer does Parzival appear as a naive innocent. He is able to listen to the distress of another, Queen Condwiramurs, and comes to her defense. The enemy that he overthrows is sent to report to Cunneware to wipe out the dishonour that he shares with her. Faultlessly, Parzival restores Condwiramurs' kingdom to order. He wins her for his bride, and "in his hands, the honour of the whole Order of Chivalry is in safe keeping." He has "overcome the impetuous exuberance of youth and [has] acquired the ability to act out of sound judgment."

Parzival rides out to learn about his mother, not knowing that she is dead. He is "destined now to suffer great anguish, but at times also honour and joy." Riding aimlessly, thinking of the woman he loves, Parzival travels so far "that a bird would have been hard put to it to fly the distance he rode that day." He arrives at the castle of Anfortas, the suffering king, where he witnesses the procession of "a thing called 'The Gral.'" Parzival watches the magnificence and wonder of it all. Remaining 'true to the dictates of good breeding," he refrains from asking questions, thinking that if he stays there long enough he will "learn unasked how matters stand." He is presented with a sword and continues to remain silent, but "alas that he asked no Question then! ... For when he was given the sword it was to prompt him to ask a Question" that his host may be rid of his suffering. Anfortas is to be healed by the asking of a Question.

When the Gral is carried from the room, Parzival catches a glimpse of "the most handsome old man he had ever seen ... whose hair ... was more silvery even than hoar-frost." This is Titurel, the guardian of the Gral. Parzival passes a night of anguish and awakens to a deserted castle. Thinking that the whole company has ridden out, he rides after them. The drawbridge is quickly drawn up after him, and he is cursed: "Damn you, wherever the sun lights your path! ... You silly goose! Why didn't you open your gob and ask my lord the Question?"

Parzival encounters Sigune for the second time, and she tells him the story of the people whose castle he has left and of the magic of the sword he was given. Seeing Parzival with Anfortas' sword, Sigune believes that he asked the Question that would rid Anfortas of his suffering. Learning that Parzival "could not be bothered to ask in the very presence of the Gral," she curses him as a dishonourable person. He should have had compassion on his host and inquired about his suffering. Parzival should have acknowledged the suffering of Anfortas, but he failed to do so. With great remorse for being "slow to ask the Question as he sat beside the sorrowing king," Parzival parts from Sigune. Once again Sigune reveals something of his nature to Parzival.

In searching for his mother, Parzival enters a realm that he does not understand and will only gain conscious knowledge of after he endures suffering. When Parzival entered Anfortas' castle, he had to remove his armour and put on a "cloak of cloth- of-gold" that belonged to the Princess of the Gral, indicating that "he was now called upon to develop a different state of consciousness from that required in his everyday life."[242] The bleeding lance that the squire carried around the room "can be regarded as an image of the king's misdirected will life, which had brought such sorrow to the community, while the sword is an indication of a faculty which he had to forfeit through his failure as Grail King,"[243] the faculty of inspiration.

After Parzival leaves Sigune, he begins to compensate for his earlier mistakes. He proves Jeschute's innocence and returns her to Orilus' favour. Orilus must also go to Arthur's court and report to Cunneware, who is his sister. Her tent is above a brook "which Rudolf Steiner refers to as the well of inspiration where the Grail sword could be re-welded and which was guarded by"[244] Cunneware. Parzival also avenges the dishonour that Cunneware suffered due to him and is able to face King Arthur and Queen Gywnevere with honor.

One spring when an unseasonal snow falls, when the world of the senses still sleeps, Parzival comes to a spot where a goose, wounded by a falcon, has shed three drops of blood. For Parzival, Condwiramurs is mirrored in the colors of the red blood against the white snow. He falls into a trance; "his thoughts concerning the Gral and this semblance of the Queen both afflicted him sorely." He becomes dominated by the sense world that is covered by a blanket of snow. Gawan is able to free Parzival from his spell, breaking his picture-memories, and allowing him to move forward. He is confronted by Cundrie who curses him, comparing him to a viper's fang; he failed to show compassion and does not deserve the sword he has been given. Her words mortify Parzival, and he feels a deep sense of shame. The Gral becomes his goal, "from which nothing shall sever" him until the end of his days. In his despair he questions: "Alas, what is God?" and renounces his service to Him.

Leaving Arthur's court in search of the Gral, Parzival has to find a new relationship to the spiritual world. The first stage of his self-development ended when he won Condwiramurs. With the suffering of the loss of happiness, the grief of unsatisfied love and shame, Parzival completes the second stage.[245]

Parzival travels through the country defending himself in many battles. The sword from Anfortas is once shattered and made whole again by "the virtues of the well." "This implies that he has now learned the rightful use of this weapon."[246] He meets again with Sigune, tells her of his sorrows to which she offers helpful advice, and sends him in pursuit of Cundrie. Through her guidance, Parzival acquires the horse of a knight from Munsalvaesche, a Gral horse. He comes upon an old knight with a grizzled beard whose words soften his stern attitude towards God, and he cries out: "If God's power is so great that it can guide horses and other beasts and people, too, than I will praise His power." Re-establishing his relationship to the spiritual world, Parzival comes upon the cell of the hermit, Trevrizent. Here he learns of "matters concerning the Gral that have been hidden," the deeper mysteries of Christianity.

Parzival recognizes that he is guilty of a crime in killing Ither, which he did when he was "dull of understanding." He also learns that his mother "died of anguish" for him when he left her.

Titurel, the First King of the Gral, has grown too old to serve as King, but was able to give wise counsel. His grandson, Anfortas, becomes King after him, but he fails to uphold his obligations as Gral King. For this he has to suffer until a knight comes and asks the Question, at which time he will be healed but will no longer be King.

Titurel, the aged father of the Gral lineage, the King of wisdom, is the great teacher. The figure of Enoch reappears in Titurel. Anfortas is the King of suffering, and in him the figure of Job reappears. The passing of the Gral from Titurel to Anfortas is a mirroring of the passing of humanity from the Atlantean to the Post-Atlantean era. As the succession of the Gral king passes from the first to the second guardian, mankind is led over a threshold, heading towards freedom.[247]

Parzival reveals to Trevrizent that he is the knight who failed to ask the Question. Trevrizent sees him as a man whose compassion has been betrayed by "the five senses Gad had given him when they shut off their aid' from him. When Parzival leaves the hermit a fortnight later, Trevrizent says: "Give me your sins." He absolves Parzival of his sins.

Throughout the story of Parzival, the relationship he has with Gawan is slowly developed. Unknowingly, they encounter each other in combat. When they discover who they are fighting, Parzival cries out, "I have vanquished myself" and Gawan replies, "If your heart be true, you have subdued yourself." Parzival regains control of his destiny, and they recognize their interdependence with each other. In the consciousness soul age "the human being cannot rely on his own strength alone, he needs to unite his Forces at the right moment with others who are developing spiritual consciousness."[248]

After a union with his brother Feirefiz, Parzival once again meets with Cundrie. She kneels before him and reveals to him that he is to be Lord of the Gral. Through steadfast striving, Parzival has "won through to peace of soul and outlived cares to have joy." Parzival reveals the teaching he had received from Trevrizent "that no man could ever win the Gral by force 'except the one who is summoned there by God.' The news spread to every land that it was not to be won by force, with the result that many abandoned the Quest of the Gral and all that went with it, and that is why it is hidden to this day."

Cundrie leads Parzival and Feirefiz to Anfortas, who receives them joyfully as well as with great anguish. Asking where the Gral is kept, Parzival genuflects in its direction to the glory of the Trinity, praying that the affliction of the man of sorrows be taken from him. Then rising to his full height he added: "Dear Uncle, what ails you?"

"Through his many trials Parzival had developed his capacities of judgment, of compassion, and of steadfastness to a high degree, and, since meeting with Trevrizent, he had united himself with the life-giving power of Christ. His words could now pour forth the forces of healing."[249] Parzival is recognized as "King and Sovereign."

In the consciousness soul epoch the "loss of spiritual wisdom and the coming of materialism were necessary so that out of the void man could awaken his own powers to regain the knowledge he had lost. In this respect we can consider Parzival as a forerunner of our time."[250] Although he is called to the Gral, Parzival must develop himself to earn the right to his position. He must take his own development in hand, so that he is able to stand before Anfortas and truly see him, to recognize the "I" of him and then ask the Question. This is the task of the Aryan epoch.

As a result of the bitter agony that gentle Anfortas suffered for so long, and because "the Question was withheld from him for such a time, the members of the Gral Company are now forever averse to questioning, they do not wish to be asked about themselves." This image reveals additional indications of the relationship between people of the twentieth century. If the consciousness soul age has the task of building bridges between people consciously by true perception and recognition of the "I" of others, this is to be done without asking questions of who they are, or what their spiritual path is.

A MODERN MYTH

The evolution of humanity has been followed through the stories of the Old Testament, the Norse myths, Indian and Persian legends, the epic of Gilgamesh, the story of Osiris and Isis, the Greek myths, including the Iliad and the Odyssey, the Aeneid, the story of Romulus and Remus, and on to the Arthurian legends, with the story of Parzival leading into the consciousness soul age. But what of the consciousness soul age? What will a story of this age reflect? As the fifth Post-Atlantean epoch is a reflection of the third Post-Atlantean epoch, Rudolf Steiner sets up a new Isis myth against the old Osiris-Isis myth as a story for this age.

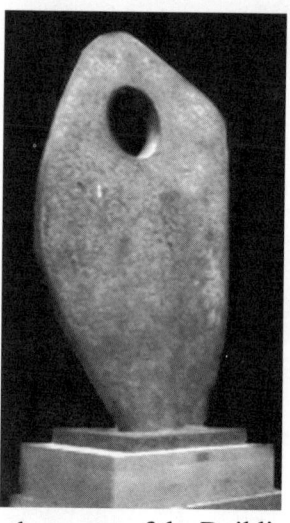

In the age of scientific profundity, upon a hill in spiritual seclusion, a Building was erected which was closed to no one and opened to all. Few people saw the Building nor what it represented. A statue stood in the centre of the Building, a statue representing a Group of beings. One was the Representative of Man, and the others were Luciferic and Ahrimanic figures. The statue, however, was in fact a veil for an invisible statue, the new Isis, the Isis of a new age. People did not notice the invisible statue. They thought that the statue signified something, but in so saying, they completely misunderstood all that underlay it, for the figures did not signify anything but were already what they appeared to be. Behind the figure was a real new Isis. The few who saw the new Isis found that she was asleep. Below the statue was an inscription: "I am Man, I am the Past, the Present and the Future. Every mortal should lift my veil."

A visitor repeatedly approached the sleeping Isis, and she saw him as her benefactor, and she loved him. The new Isis had an offspring and thought the visitor was the father. He, too, saw himself as the father, but he was not. This visitor was none other than the new Typhon, and he believed he could increase his power if he took possession of the new Isis. Isis knew nothing of the nature of her offspring. She moved it about, dragging it into other lands, believing that she must do so. Dragging it about, the new offspring fell apart into fourteen pieces through the power of the world.

The new Typhon, when he heard of this, gathered together the fourteen pieces, and with all the knowledge of natural scientific profundity, he made a being, a single whole out of the fourteen pieces. In this being there were only the mechanical laws of the machine. This being could reproduce itself fourteenfold, and a reflection of Typhon was given to each piece; each of the fourteen offspring of the new Isis had a face resembling the new Typhon. Isis knew that she herself had brought about the miraculous change of her offspring, for she had dragged it about. There came a day when, in its genuine form, she could accept it again from the elemental spirits of nature. As she received her true offspring, which only through an illusion had been stamped into the offspring of Typhon, she gained clairvoyant vision. Even though she was the new Isis, she still wore the cow-horns of ancient Egypt. Through the power of her clairvoyance, Typhon, or Mercury, was obliged to set a crown on her head, where once the old Isis received the crown which Horus had seized from her. Her new crown was merely a paper crown, covered with all sorts of writings of a profoundly scientific nature. Now she wore two crowns, the cow-horns and the paper crown embellished with all the wisdom of scientific profundity.

Through the strength of her clairvoyance there arose in her the significance of the Mystery of Golgotha. Through this the cow-horns grasped the paper crown and changed it into a golden crown.[251]

"Even though the power of action which is bound up with the new Isis statue is at first only weak, exploring and attempting, it is to be the starting point of something that is deeply justified in the impulses of the modern age, deeply justified in what this age is meant to become and must become."[252]

EPILOGUE

The bearers of the fifth Post-Atlantean epoch descended from those Atlanteans who had been least affected by what took place in the four preceding epochs. They transmitted the heritage of the Atlantean civilization in their own way. They knew the spiritual worlds from their own experiences and could speak of it. Thus, there arose a world of stories about spiritual beings and events. The fairy-tales and sagas of the peoples came from these real spiritual experiences. Mythologies reveal traces of what the initiates in the Mysteries were able to make known to mankind.[253] The facts of cosmic evolution and the development of consciousness are revealed in myths, stories, and legends.

At the present time the dawn of the sixth Post-Atlantean epoch is already appearing,

> for whatever is to emerge at a certain time in human evolution, will always be slowly maturing in the preceding time. One thing can even now begin to evolve in its initial stages, namely the finding of the thread which will unite the two spheres that claim man's devotion – the material civilization, and life in the spiritual world. To this end it is necessary on the one hand that the results of spiritual seership be received and understood, and on the other, that in man's observations and experiences of the sense-world the revelations of the Spirit be recognized. The sixth civilization-epoch will bring to full development the harmony between the two.[254]

In the sixth Post-Atlantean epoch the Old Persian epoch will appear again, and the Old Indian epoch will appear in a new form in the seventh period. As the caste system developed in ancient India, another grouping of people will appear in the seventh Post-Atlantean era. While the division in the first period was effected by authority, "in the seventh period men will group themselves according to objective points of view.... The salvation of humanity lies in division into objective groups, and they will even be able to combine division of labor with equality of rights. Human society will appear as a wonderful harmony. ....Thus ancient India will appear again."[255]

At the end of the seventh Post-Atlantean epoch, there will again be a period of pralaya, and then the earth will continue to evolve through the Jupiter, Venus, and Vulcan incarnations. Humanity will continue to evolve until, hopefully, the goal of the gods will be fulfilled. Throughout the future cycles of time, assuredly stories will continue to reveal the cosmic and evolutionary events that humanity experiences.

The End

REFERENCES

1. Rudolf Steiner, *Occult Science: An Outline* (London: Rudolf Steiner Press, 1972), 39-59.
2. Ibid., 104.
3. Rudolf Steiner, *Genesis: Secrets of the Bible Story of Creation* (London: Rudolf Steiner Press, 1959), 17.
4. Steiner, *Occult Science*, 161.
5. Steiner, *Genesis*, 44.
6. Rudolf Steiner, *Cosmic Memory: Atlantis and Lemuria* (New York: Anthroposophic Press, 1971), 174-183.
7. Steiner, *Occult Science*, 118.
8. Steiner, *Genesis*, 35.
9. Steiner, *Occult Science*, 129.
10. Steiner, *Cosmic Memory*, 187.
11. Steiner, *Occult Science*, 130.
12. Steiner, *Genesis*, 35-37.
13. Steiner, *Occult Science*, 130.
14. Steiner, *Cosmic Memory*, 186.
15. Steiner, *Occult Science*, 132-136.
16. Ibid., 138.
17. Steiner, *Cosmic Memory*, 198-199.
18. Steiner, *Occult Science*, 113.
19. Ibid., 139.
20. Ibid., 140-141.
21. Rudolf Steiner, *Egyptian Myths and Mysteries*, (New York: Anthroposophic Press, 1971), 52.
22. Steiner, *Genesis*, 37-38.
23. Steiner, *Cosmic Memory*, 196-197.
24. Steiner, *Genesis*, 88-91.
25. Steiner, *Occult Science*, 148.
26. Steiner, *Genesis*, 92.
27. Steiner, *Occult Science*, 149-151.
28. Steiner, *Genesis,* 28-29.

29. Steiner, *Egyptian Myths and Mysteries*, 54-55.
30. Ibid., 58.
31. Steiner, *Cosmic Memory*, 208.
32. Steiner, *Occult Science*, 155.
33. Steiner, *Cosmic Memory*, 209-211.
34. Steiner, *Egyptian Myths and Mysteries*, 44.
35. Steiner, *Genesis*, 34.
36. Ibid., 57-58.
37. Ibid., 16-21.
38. Ibid., 26.
39. Kevin Crossley-Holland, *The Norse Myths* (London: Andre Deutsch, 1980), 3.
40. Steiner, *Occult Science*, 164.
41. Ibid., 162.
42. Steiner, *Genesis*, 95.
43. Ibid., 96.
44. Steiner, *Occult Science*, 165.
45. Ibid., 166.
46. Ibid., 171.
47. Emil Bock, *Genesis: Creation and the Patriarchs* (Edinburgh: Floris Books, 1983), 32.
48. Steiner, *Egyptian Myths and Mysteries*, 20.
49. Steiner, *Genesis*, 116.
50. Ibid., 105.
51. Ibid., 69.
52. Ibid., 109.
53. Bock, *Genesis*, 25.
54. Steiner, *Genesis*, 133.
55. Ibid., 124-125.
56. Ibid., 128.
57. Ibid., 131.
58. Steiner, *Occult Science*, 180.
59. Steiner, *Cosmic Memory*, 90.
60. Ibid., 94-95.
61. Bock, *Genesis*, 38.
62. Steiner, *Genesis*, 111.
63. Stewart Easton, *Man and World in Light of Anthroposophy*, (New York: The Antrhroposophic Press, 1975), 204-205.
64. Ibid., 28.
65. Steiner, *Occult Science*, 192.

66. Steiner, *Cosmic Memory*, 71-86.
67. Steiner, *Occult Science*, 190.
68. Crossley-Holland, "The Creation," in *The Norse Myths*, 5.
69. Ibid., xxvi.
70. Ibid., "The Lay of Thrym," 70.
71. Ibid., "Hyndla's Poem," 100.
72. Padriac Colum, "Iduna and Her Apples," in *The Children of Odin* (Edinburgh: Floris Books, 1993), 13.
73. Ibid., "The Building of the Wall," 6.
74. Ibid., 77.
75. Ibid., 17.
76. Ibid, "Iduna and Her Apples," 13.
77. Ibid., "How Frey Won Gerda," 51.
78. Ibid., "The Valkyrie," 173.
79. Ibid., "Odin Goes to Mimir's Well," 77.
80. Crossley-Holland, "Lord of the Gallows," in *The Norse Myths*, 15.
81. Colum, "Odin Wins for Men the Magic Mead," *The Children of Odin*, 90.
82. Picard, *Tales of the Norse Gods and Heroes* (London: Oxford University Press, 1961), 87.
83. Colum, "Odin Faces an Evil Man," *The Children of Odin*, 82.
84. Picard, *Tales of the Norse Gods and Heroes*, 82.
85. Ibid., 120.
86. Crossley-Holland, "The Song of Rig," in *The Norse Myths*, 18.
87. Steiner, *Cosmic Memory*, 72.
88. Colum, *The Children of Odin*, 230
89. Colum, "The Twilight of the Gods," in *The Children of Odin*, 265.
90. Picard, *Tales of Norse Gods and Heroes*, 152.
91. Bock, *Genesis*, 49-50
92. Ibid., 50.
93. Ibid., 50-51.
94. Ibid., 51.
95. Steiner, *Cosmic Memory*, 42.
96. Ibid., 43.
97. Bock, *Genesis*, 53.
98. Steiner, *Cosmic Memory*, 50-58.

99. Ibid., 53.
100. Steiner, *Occult Science*, 196.
101. Bock, *Genesis*, 54.
102. Steiner, *Cosmic Memory*, 54.
103. Steiner, *Occult Science*, 194.
104. Bock, *Genesis*, 58.
105. Ibid., 60-61.
106. Steiner, *Cosmic Memory*, 46.
107. Steiner, *Genesis*, 117.
108. Steiner, *Occult Science*, 197.
109. Steiner, *Egyptian Myths and Mysteries*, 109.
110. Steiner, *Occult Science*, 197.
111. Ibid., 198.
112. Bock, *Genesis*, 68.
113. Ibid., 71.
114. Ibid., 74.
115. Hackin, *Asiatic Mythology*, (New York: Crescent Books, 1985), 134.
116. Bock, *Genesis*, 79-82.
117. Ibid., 77-85.
118. Ibid., 85.
119. Steiner, *Cosmic Memory*, 63-64.
120. Bock, *Genesis*, 89.
121. Steiner, *Occult Science*, 204.
122. Easton, *Man and World in the Light of Anthroposophy*, 37.
123. Steiner, *Occult Science*, 202-203.
124. Steiner, *Egyptian Myths and Mysteries*, 22-23.
125. Easton, *Man and World in the Light of Anthroposophy*, 158-159.
126. Steiner, *Egyptian Myths and Mysteries*, 6.
127. Easton, *Man and World in the Light of Anthroposophy*, 30.
128. J.E.B. Gray, *Indian Tales and Legends*, (London: Oxford University Press, 1965), 89-154.
129. Hackin, *Asiatic Mythology*, 140-141.
130. Gray, *Indian Tales and Legends*, 32-33.
131. Ibid., 165-171.
132. Virgina Haviland, *Favorite Fairy Tales Told in India*, (London: The Bodley Head, Ltd., 1973), 36-52.
133. Easton, *Man and World in the Light of Anthroposophy*, 37.
134. Steiner, *Occult Science*, 205-206.

135. Easton, *Man and World in the Light of Anthroposophy*, 33.
136. Bock. *Genesis*, 95.
137. Steiner, *Occult Science*, 208.
138. Easton, *Man and World in the Light of Anthroposophy*, 31-33.
139. Steiner, *Occult Science*, 206-207.
140. Easton, *Man and World in the Light of Anthroposophy*, 33.
141. Steiner, *Egyptian Myths and Mysteries*, 23.
142. Easton, *Man and World in the Light of Anthroposophy*, 34.
143. Bock, *Genesis*, 9.
144. John Hinnells, *Persian Mythology* (London: Hamlyn, 1973), 56.
145. Steiner, *Egyptian Myths and Mysteries*, 96-97.
146. Veronica Ions, *The World's Mythology* (London: Hamlyn, 1974). 66.
147. Hinnells, *Persian Mythology*, 62.
148. Ions, *The World's Mythology*, 66.
149. Ibid., 55.
150. Bock, *Genesis*, 89-98.
151. N.K. Sanders, *The Epic of Gilgamesh* (England: Penguin Books, 1977).
152. Easton, *Man and World in Light of Anthroposophy*, 48.
153. Steiner, *Occult Science*, 210.
154. Steiner, *Egyptian Myths and Mysteries*, 154.
155. Steiner, *Occult Science*, 209.
156. Steiner, *Egyptian Myths and Mysteries*, 98.
157. Steiner, *Occult Science*, 210.
158. Ions, *The World's Mythology*, 30.
159. Easton, *Man and World in the Light of Anthroposophy*, 39.
160. Ions, *The World's Mythology*, 28-3.
161. This myth is retold from two sources: (1) Steiner, *Egyptian Myths and Mysteries*, pages 15-23. and (2) Ions, *The World's Mythology*, pages 33-34.
162. Steiner, *Occult Science*, 209.
163. Easton, *Man and World in Light of Anthroposophy*, 41.
164. Steiner, *Egyptian Myths and Mysteries*, 24.
165. Steiner, *Egyptian Myths and Mysteries*, 59.
166. Steiner, *Ancient Myths*, 17-18.
167. Steiner, *Egyptian Myths and Mysteries*, 65.

168. Ibid., 121.
169. Steiner, *Ancient Myths*, 19.
170. Easton, *Man and World in Light of Anthroposophy*, 38-40.
171. Donald Mackenzie, *Egyptian Myth and Legend*, 327-330.
172. Bock, *Genesis*, 97.
173. Ibid., 107.
174. Ibid., 104.
175. Ibid., 110.
176. Ibid., 115.
177. Ibid., 135.
178. Ibid., 122.
179. Easton, *Man and World in Light of Anthroposophy*, 50.
180. Ibid., 40, 49.
181. Emil Bock, *Genesis*, 137.
182. Ibid., 138.
183. Ibid., 109-110.
184. Ibid., 142.
185. Ibid., 144.
186. Ibid., 145
187. Ibid., 148.
188. Ibid., 154.
189. Ibid., 152.
190. Ibid., 158.
191. Ibid., 162.
192. Ibid., 169.
193. Ibid., 169-170.
194. Ibid., 175.
195. Ibid., 171.
196. Colum, *The Golden Fleece,* (New York: Macmillan Publishing, 1921), 110-114.
197. Steiner, *Egyptian Myths and Mysteries,* 117-118.
198. This myth is retold from two sources: (1) *The Golden Fleece* and (2) *The Heroes*
199. Picard, *The Iliad of Homer*
200. Stuart Gordon, *Encyclopedia of Myths and Legends,* (London: Headline Book Publishing, 1994), 7.
201. Bock, *Genesis*, 143.
202. Barbara Leonie Picard, *The Odyssey of Homer* (London: Oxford University, 1967)
203. Picard, *Tales of the Norse Gods and Heroes*, 181.

204. Picard, *The Odyssey of Homer*, 38.
205. Colum, *The Golden Fleece* (New York, Macmillan, 1921), 228-236.
206. Virgil, *The Aeneid* (England: Penguin, 1958)
207. Picard, *The Iliad of Homer*, 4.
208. Steiner, *Egyptian Myths and Mysteries*, 24.
209. Easton, *Man and World in Light of Anthroposophy*, 74.
210. Steiner, *Egyptian Myths and Mysteries*, 101.
211. Steiner, *Occult Science*, 214.
212. Pierre Grimal, *The Civilization of Rome*, (London: George Allen and Unwin, Ltd., 1963), 37-40.
213. Ibid., 38-39.
214. Ibid., 41.
215. Easton, *Man and World in Light of Anthroposophy*, 55.
216. Ibid., 78-80.
217. Ibid., 51-52.
218. Ibid., 57.
219. Ibid., 52.
220. Ibid., 56.
221. Sir Thomas Mallory, *Le Morte d'Arthur* (New York: Bramhall House, 1962), 305.
222. Ibid., 302.
223. Ibid., 26.
224. Picard, *Tales of the Norse Gods and Heroes*, 184.
225. Picard, *Stories of King Arthur and His Knights*, (London: Oxford University, 1965), 17.
226. Mallory, *Le Morte d'Arthur*, 380.
227. H. A. Guerber, *Middle Ages: Myths and Legends*, (London: Senate, 1994), 290.
228. Eileen Hutchins, *Parzival, an Introduction*, (London: Temple Lodge Press, 1987), 8.
229. Retelling of the King Arthur story is based upon *Le Morte d'Arthur* by Sir Thomas Mallory.
230. Steiner, *Egyptian Myths and Mysteries*, 84-85.
231. Steiner, *Occult Science*, 218-219.
232. Easton, *Man and World in Light of Anthroposophy*, 88-100.
233. Steiner, *Egyptian Myths and Mysteries*, 7.
234. Ibid., 8.
235. Ibid., 9.
236. Easton, *Man and World in Light of Anthroposophy*, 102.

237. Steiner, *Egyptian Myths and Mysteries*, 24-25.
238. Easton, *Man and World in Light of Anthroposophy*, 94-115.
239. Ibid., 111
240. Wolfram von Eschenbach, *Parzival* (England: Penguin, 1980)
241. Ibid., 31.
242. Ibid., 41.
243. Ibid., 42.
244. Ibid., 43.
245. Ibid., 48.
246. Ibid., 55.
247. Bock, *Genesis*, 78.
248. von Eschenbach, *Parzival*, 80.
249. Ibid., 85.
250. Ibid., 91.
251. Steiner, *Ancient Myths*, 37-40.
252. Ibid., 40.
253. Steiner, *Occult Science*, 219.
254. Ibid., 221.
255. Steiner, *Egyptian Myths and Mysteries*, 6.

BIBLIOGRAPHY

The New English Bible, Oxford University Press, 1970.

Bock, Emil, *Genesis: Creation and the Patriarchs*, Floris Books, Edinburgh, 1983.

Colum, Padraic, *The Children of Odin*, Floris Books, Edinburgh, 1993.

_____, *The Golden Fleece*, Macmillan Publishing Co., Inc., New York, 1921.

Crossley-Holland, Kevin, *The Norse Myths*, Andre Deutsch, London, 1980.

Easton, Stewart C., *Man and World in Light of Anthroposophy*, The Anthroposophic Press, New York, 1975.

Gordon, Stuart, *The Encyclopeida of Myths and Legends*, Headline Book Publishing, London, 1994.

Gray, J.E.B., *Indian Tales and Legends*, Oxford University Press, London, 1965.

Grimal, Pierre, *The Civilization of Rome*, George Allen and Unwin Ltd., London, 1963.

Guerber, H.A., *Middle Ages, Myths and Legends*, Senate, London, 1994.

Hackin, J., *Asiatic Mythology*, Crescent Books, New York, 1985.

Haviland, Virginia, *Favorite Fairy Tales Told in India*, The Bodley Head Ltd., London, 1973.

Hinnells, John R., *Persian Mythology*, Hamlyn, London, 1973.

Hutchins, Eileen, *Parzival, an Introduction*, Temple Lodge Press, London, 1987.

Ions, Veronica, *The World's Mythology*, Hamlyn, London, 1974.

ILLUSTRATIONS

Cover – Relief depicting the Battle of the Centaurs, Michaelangelo, 1492.
Page 5 – Medieval etching of man looking behind the stars.
Page 12 – Painting, God giving life to Adam, Sistine Chapel, Michaelangelo, 1508-12.
Page 17 – Painting, Adam and Eve sent from Paradise.
Page 18 – Carving from the prow of a Viking ship.
Page 22 – Mayan symbol for life emerging after the great flood.
Page 27 – Noah and the Ark from the Nuremberg Bible.
Page 30 – National symbol of India, erected by Emporer Ashaka in 3 B.C.
Page 33 – Patriarch of Babylonia.
Page 36 – Frieze of Gilgamesh.
Page 40 – Copied from Egyptian papryus painting.
Page 42 – Osiris and Goddesses from the Temple of Seti, Abydos.
Page 44 – (top) Isis from a 19th Century mural in Seti's Temple.
Page 44 – (bottom) Death mask of Tutankhamun.
Page 45 – Sculpture of Abraham from the Catherdral at Chartres.
Page 51 – Stele depicting Joseph's brothers selling him into slavery.
Page 53 – Greek Amphora depicting Ajax and Achilles playing Droughts.
Page 59 – Taken from a mosaic depicting Aeneas hunting.
Page 60 – Painting of Moses with the Ten Commandments.
Page 61 – The Parthanon in Athens, Ictinus and Callicrates, architects, 447-432 B.C.
Page 62 – The wolf giving suckle to Romulus and Remus.
Page 65 – King Arthur, taken from a medieval illustration.
Page 74 – Frieze depicting the travails of Parcival.
Page 78 – Sculpture of Knights on the Crusade, from Chartres.
Page 80 – Sculpture "Single Form," by Barbara Hepworth, 1961-2.
Page 83 – Bronze sculpture by Myron, "The Discobolus."